Margaret Pict[o...

Understanding Parenthood and Child Care

Illustrated by Doreen Lang

Blackie

To Mum and Dad

© Margaret Picton 1980
First Published 1980
ISBN 0 216 90738 1

Symbol on pages 163 and 172 reproduced by permission of
The Controller of Her Majesty's Stationery Office

BLACKIE & SON LTD
Bishopbriggs · Glasgow G64 2NZ
•
Furnival House · 14-18 High Holborn · London WC1V 6BX

Printed in Great Britain

Contents

How our bodies develop

There is one thing we all have in common. Each and every one of us started life as a new-born baby. We gradually grew in size, and as we grew changes took place in our bodies. These changes were brought about by chemicals called *hormones*.

Hormones are fluids or secretions produced by the *endocrine glands*. Hormones pass into the bloodstream. They are not excreted (expelled) from the body through openings or ducts, like sweat, saliva and tears. Endocrine or ductless glands are found in various parts of the body, and the hormone secreted (produced) by each gland has a particular job to perform if our bodies are to grow and develop properly. Here are some of the endocrine glands.

The thyroid gland in the neck produces THYROXIN. This hormone influences the temperament and physical development of the body.

The pancreas gland secretes INSULIN. This hormone helps to burn up sugar in the blood.

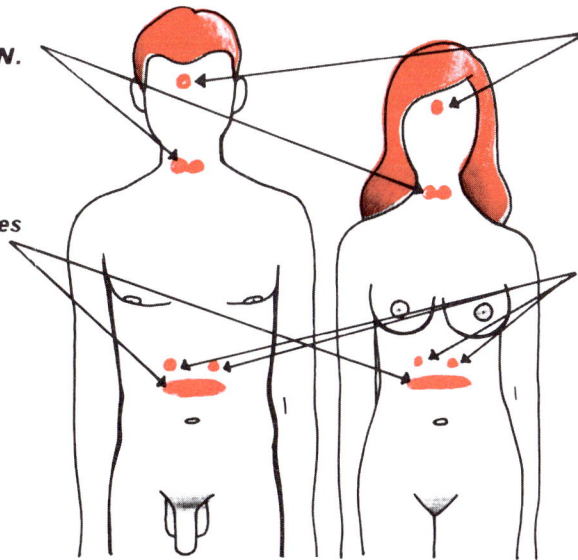

The pituitary gland is situated at the base of the brain. It secretes several hormones which regulate growth. This gland helps to control the other endocrine glands and is sometimes called the "master gland".

The adrenal glands above each kidney produce ADRENALIN. This hormone is released in times of stress. It can make the heart beat faster and the blood pressure rise.

The sex glands produce hormones but they are not ductless glands. Both male and female sex glands have a duct or tube leading to the outside of the body.

The male sex glands are called *testes* or *testicles*. A boy has two testes which are suspended between the legs in a fleshy bag called the *scrotum*. The testes produce *spermatozoa* or sperm. They also secrete hormones which control the emotional and physical development of the body.

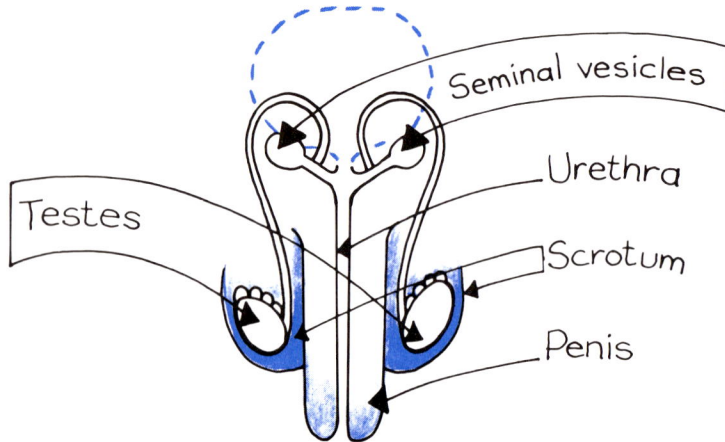

The female sex glands are called *ovaries*. They are situated in the abdomen or lower part of the trunk. The ovaries produce eggs or *ova*. They also secrete hormones which control the emotional and physical development of the body.

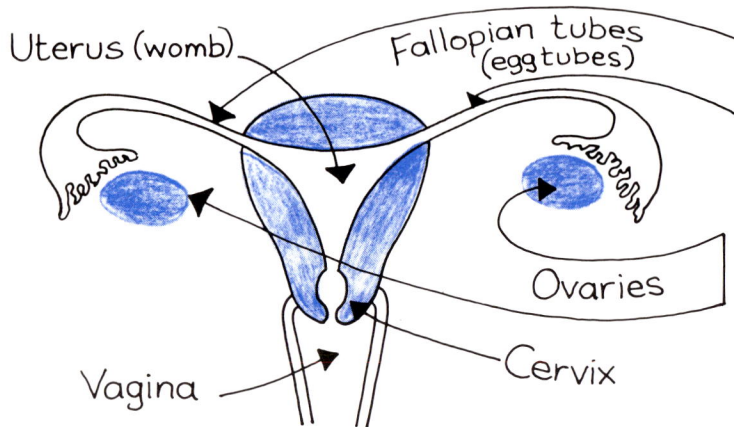

Sex hormones are present in the body from childhood but it is during adolescence that they increase and play an important part in bodily growth and behaviour. *Adolescence* and *puberty* are names given to the period of change from childhood to adulthood.

As a girl grows in size, her body develops in preparation for motherhood. The *mammary glands* or breasts enlarge, making the chest appear bigger. The hips become wider in preparation for pregnancy and childbirth, and hair starts to grow across the pubic bone and underneath the arms. These outward changes may become apparent when a girl is around 10 years old, or they may not be noticeable until she is in her early teens. Around the same time, changes occur inside a girl's body. The ovaries grow in size and start to produce mature ova. An ovum or single egg is shed each month by one or other of the ovaries. This is called *ovulation*. The ovum passes down the *Fallopian tube* into the *uterus*, and is discharged from the body, along with the lining of the uterus, in a slow trickle of blood. The uterus wall then starts to grow another lining in readiness for the release of the next ovum. This cycle takes about 28 days and is called *menstruation*. The beginning of menstruation is a normal stage in the development from girlhood to womanhood, and is brought about by hormones in the sex glands.

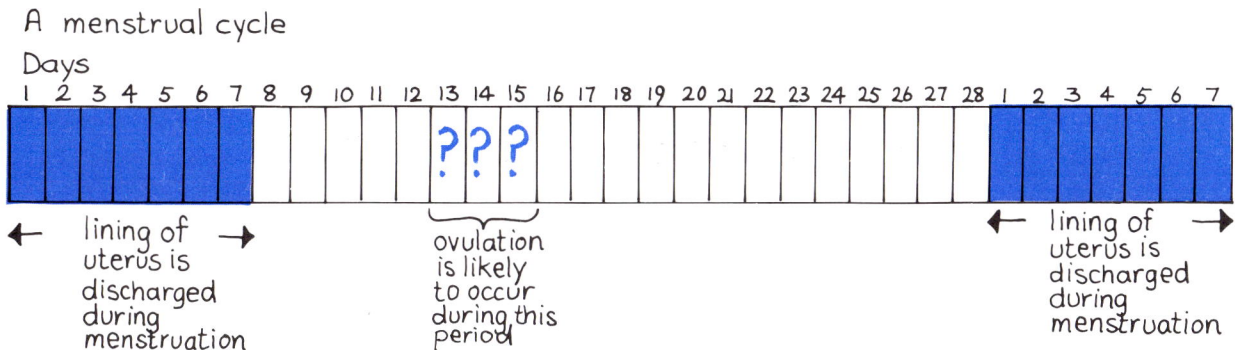

A menstrual cycle

Days

1 2 3 4 5 6 7 8 9 10 11 12 13 14 15 16 17 18 19 20 21 22 23 24 25 26 27 28 1 2 3 4 5 6 7

? ? ?

← lining of → uterus is discharged during menstruation

ovulation is likely to occur during this period

← lining of → uterus is discharged during menstruation

When menstruation becomes regular, a girl is fertile, and capable of becoming pregnant if an ovum is fertilized. Menstruation continues every month, except during pregnancy, until she becomes too old to bear children. The *menopause*, or change in life, is the period when a woman's reproductive life ceases. This usually happens around the age of 50. Menstruation may become irregular for a while before stopping altogether. Occasionally the menopause can produce unpleasant effects, such as sleeplessness, irritability and depression, and some women suffer from sudden hot flushes. These conditions can be caused by a drop in the level of the sex hormone, **oestrogen**, which is secreted by the ovaries. Treatment can be prescribed by a doctor if necessary.

As a boy grows in size, his body develops in preparation for manhood. His shoulders become broader, and his body stronger and more masculine. Hair starts to grow across the pubic bone, on the chest and eventually on the face also. His voice begins to break and becomes deeper. These outward changes may become apparent when a boy is around 13 years old, or they may not be noticeable until he is in his middle teens. Around the same time, changes occur inside a boy's body. The testes start to produce sperm, which are stored in two reservoirs called **seminal vesicles**. During puberty, there may be regular discharges of sperm from the penis, in a whitish fluid called **semen**. This usually happens during sleep and can be accompanied by exciting sexual sensations, sometimes referred to as "wet dreams". This is a normal stage in the development from boyhood to manhood, and is brought about by hormones in the sex glands.

When a boy starts to produce sperm, he is fertile, and capable of fertilizing an ovum.

These physical changes during puberty can cause problems, and it is quite normal for healthy adolescents to feel tired, awkward and self-conscious about their developing bodies. They may worry unnecessarily, and become moody and unsure of their feelings. They may resent authority and this often shows itself in a defiant and critical attitude to parents. During puberty, hormones also influence emotions. Adolescent boys or girls will start to feel attracted to the opposite sex, and may experience disturbing sexual sensations that are sometimes difficult to control. This is all part of the natural development of the male and female reproductive organs.

Think and Do

1. Why is adolescence a difficult period?

2. Copy the following diagram into your notebook. Label the parts indicated.

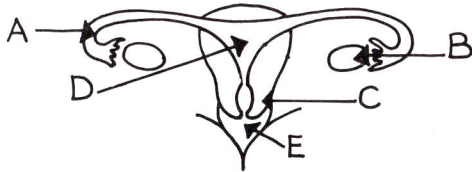

3. His name was Banting. In 1922 he made a discovery which was of immense importance to diabetics. Visit your school and local libraries and find out all you can about his life and work.

4. In your own words, explain what is meant by the following terms:
a. menstruation; ***b.*** puberty; ***c.*** "wet dreams".

5. List the physical, mental and emotional changes that occur in a boy and girl during puberty.

6. Choose a word from column B to complete each sentence in column A. Write the completed sentences in your notebook.

Column A	*Column B*
a. . . . . . . is a hormone which helps to burn up sugar in the blood.	*testes*
b. The female sex glands are called	*insulin*
c. The . . . . . . produce sperm.	*adrenalin*
d. The female monthly cycle is called	*ovaries*
e. . . . . . . is a hormone which is released by the body in times of stress.	*semen*
f. Sperm is discharged from the body in a whitish fluid called	*menstruation*

7. Copy out this crossword and complete it.

Clues across
1. Another name for adolescence.
2. The fleshy bag which holds the testes.
3. An egg.

Clues down
4. A gland in the neck.
5. When a woman's reproductive life ceases.
6. The womb.

8. Find out all you can about hormones and how they affect our bodies.

9. Are these sentences *true* or *false*?
a. The pituitary gland is the master gland.
b. The menopause is when the female monthly cycle is interrupted during pregnancy.
c. Sperm is stored in reservoirs called seminal vesicles.
d. The male sex glands are situated inside the abdomen.
e. The female monthly cycle takes about 28 days.
f. Sex hormones are present in the body from childhood.
10. Why does an adolescent often feel self-conscious and moody? Say how **a.** a family and **b.** a school can help a teenager through this stage in his development.

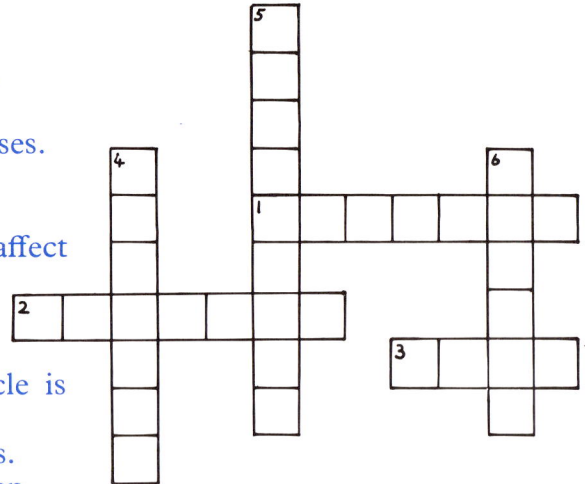

Mating and conception

When a man becomes sexually aroused, his penis grows larger. It becomes erect and hard. In mating or *coitus*, the penis is inserted inside the woman's vagina. At the climax of the mating embrace, semen is forced through the penis and into the vagina. This is called *ejaculation*. Semen contains millions of sperm. Each sperm resembles a minute tadpole, and has a head and a long tail which can propel it along with a swimming motion.

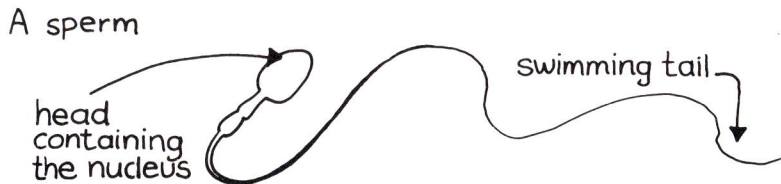

A sperm

head containing the nucleus

swimming tail

After coitus has taken place, the sperm swim into the uterus and up the Fallopian tubes. If an ovum has been released and is passing down the Fallopian tube, it will attract the sperm. One of the sperm will unite with the ovum. This is called *fertilization*. The fertilized ovum then rejects the other sperm, which eventually die. The sperm and the ovum each contain a nucleus. After fertilization has taken place, the two nuclei fuse together to form an *embryo*. The woman has now conceived or become pregnant, and will give birth to a baby approximately 266 days after conception. Menstruation will cease until several weeks after the birth of the baby, when the monthly cycle will once more return to its 28 day routine.

The fertilized ovum or embryo passes slowly along the Fallopian tube and into the uterus. This journey usually takes 3 days. During this time the embryo starts to divide. This process is called *cell division*. Cell division continues until a cluster of cells is produced. At this stage the embryo resembles a mulberry, and is called the *morulla*.

The lining of the wall of the uterus has been preparing to receive and nourish the embryo, and it is now thick and soft. The embryo eats into the lining of the uterus and attaches itself firmly to the wall by growing finger-like projections. Through these projections or "feelers" the embryo obtains nourishment from the mother's bloodstream.

The cells of the developing embryo continue to multiply by division. Some of the cells break down to form a hollow sphere, which fills with fluid. This becomes the *amniotic sac* which surrounds and protects the growing embryo while it is in the uterus. A membrane forms around the sphere or sac, and this thickens in one place and eventually develops into the *placenta* or after-birth. The remaining cell mass projects into the hollow sphere and resembles a bud on a stalk. The bud will grow into the baby, and the stalk will become the *umbilical cord* attaching the embryo to the placenta.

As the embryo grows, it develops human characteristics, and by the end of the second month (the eighth week of pregnancy), its head, face, legs and arms have been formed. The developing embryo is now referred to as the *foetus*.

Heredity

We have learned that each individual person begins life as a single cell or fertilized ovum, which then grows and divides until millions and billions of cells are formed. Though all these cells descend from the fertilized ovum, they each develop differently.

Each cell contains a nucleus and each nucleus has 46 rod-like threads called *chromosomes*, 23 coming from each parent. Chromosomes carry inherited characteristics or traits from one generation to the next. This means that any individual will inherit half of his characteristics from his mother and half from his father. For example, a person may inherit his mother's curly hair but his father's brown eyes. Mental as well as physical characteristics can be inherited, and many illnesses and disorders can also be traced to heredity.

The study of heredity is called *genetics*, and a specialist in genetic disorders is called a *geneticist*.

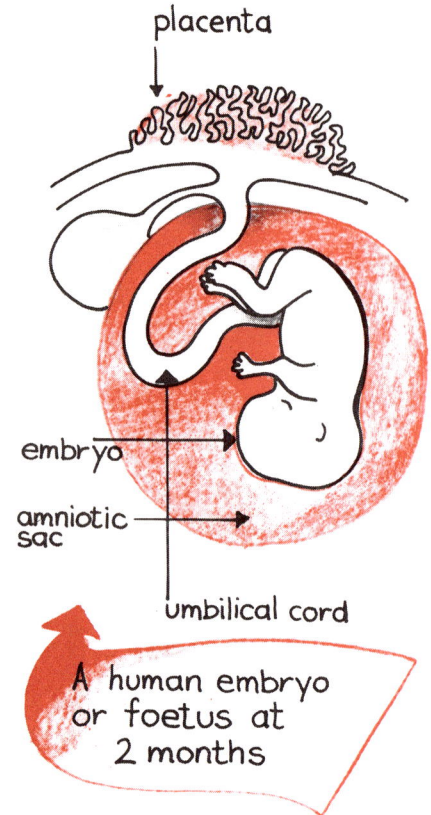

placenta

embryo

amniotic sac

umbilical cord

A human embryo or foetus at 2 months

How the sex of a child is determined

The sex of a child is determined at conception by the type of sperm which fertilizes the ovum. Each male cell carries either an X chromosome or a Y chromosome. X chromosomes produce girls and Y chromosomes produce boys.

How twins are formed

Twins can be conceived by:

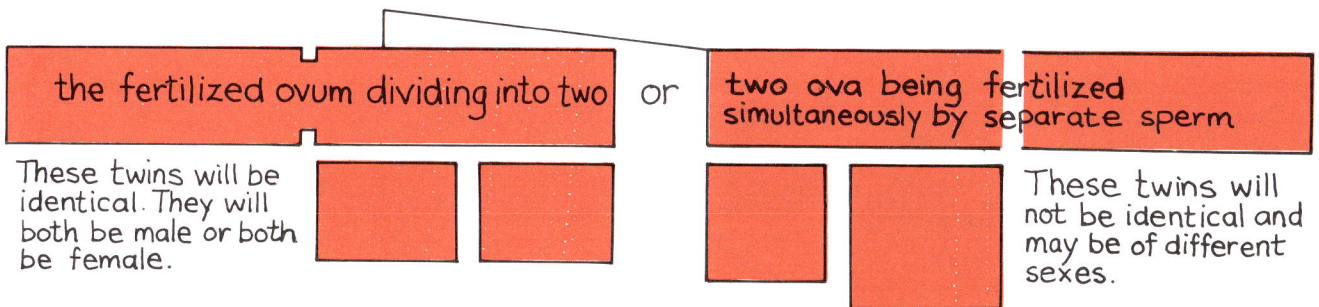

the fertilized ovum dividing into two   or   two ova being fertilized simultaneously by separate sperm

These twins will be identical. They will both be male or both be female.

These twins will not be identical and may be of different sexes.

Think and Do

1. How are twins conceived? In your own words explain the difference between identical and unidentical twins.

2. Copy the following sentences into your notebook. Say whether each one is *true* or *false*.

a. There are forty-seven chromosomes in the nucleus of each cell.

b. A fertilized ovum is called an embryo.

c. The sex of a child is determined by the sperm.

d. Identical twins are formed when two ova are fertilized simultaneously.

e. At the climax of sexual intercourse, semen is forced through the penis and into the vagina.

f. The monthly cycle ceases when a woman becomes pregnant.

3. Visit your school and local libraries and find out all you can about Gregor Johann Mendel and his work on heredity.

4. In your notebook, write a sentence about each of the following:
a. placenta;
b. umbilical cord;
c. amniotic sac.

5. Imagine that a woman conceives on July 2nd. Calculate the approximate date of the birth of her baby.

6. In your notebook, describe what is meant by the following terms:
a. cell division;
b. inherited disorder;
c. fertilization.

7. Make a list of physical and mental traits which can be inherited.

8. Copy the diagram into your notebook. Label the parts indicated.

9. Choose a word from column B to complete each sentence in column A. Write the completed sentence in your notebook.

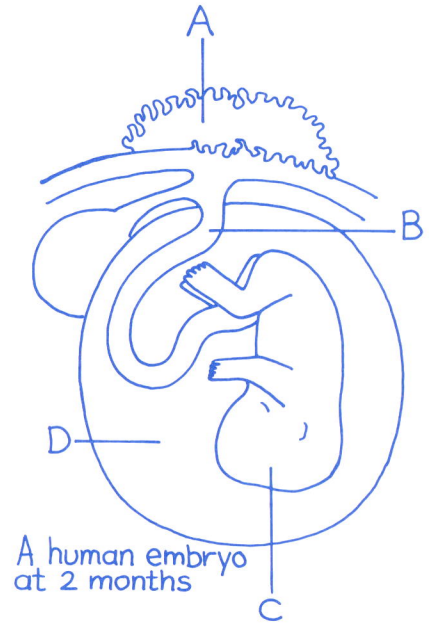

A human embryo at 2 months

Column A	Column B
a. Semen is forced through the penis during	*umbilical*
b. Each sperm and ovum contains a	*fluid*
c. The embryo develops in a sac filled with	*sperm*
d. The embryo is attached to the placenta by the . . . . . . cord.	*ejaculation*
e. The sex of the child is determined by the	*nucleus*

10. Copy out this crossword and complete it.

Clues across
1. The central or vital part of each cell.
2. A rod-like thread which carries inherited traits.
3. Embryo.

Clues down
4. The act of mating.
5. The study of heredity.
6. The period after conception and before the birth of a baby.

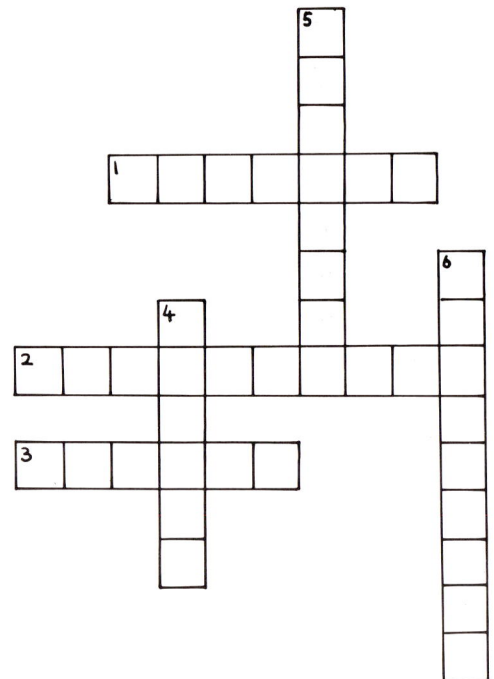

Sexual relationships and the responsibilities of starting a family

The young boy reaching manhood and the young girl maturing to womanhood will become more curious about the mechanics of sex. They will experience quite normal sexual sensations as their bodies develop, and they will feel physically attracted and attractive to one another.

Most young people start to experiment in sexual matters when they begin to "go out together", or date each other. These experiments can range from a goodnight kiss, cuddle or embrace, to caressing and touching each other's body. The physical urge to mate or make love is a powerful one, which is more easily aroused and satisfied in a young man than in a young woman. For this reason it is not wise for a girl to excite her boyfriend, or tempt him with suggestive looks, long passionate embraces or intimate caresses. She may find that she is playing with a force that is difficult to control.

In the animal kingdom, mating is purely for the purpose of procreating or reproducing the species, but to human beings making love means more than this. It is a means of expressing one's deep feelings and affection for another person, in an exciting, pleasurable and gratifying way. This expression of love only has meaning when it is within a caring and stable relationship. The young man or young woman who uses sexual intercourse purely as a means of obtaining physical satisfaction, shows a lack of control and self-respect, and a selfish disregard for the possible consequences.

There is a real danger that a person indulging in casual sexual relationships will become infected with a *venereal disease*, and will then pass the disease on to subsequent partners with whom he or she has sexual intercourse.

There is a further danger to consider. Medical opinion suggests that there is a greater chance of a female developing cancer of the cervix in later life, if she begins having sexual intercourse early on in adolescence.

1. It can be called **V.D.** for short.
2. **V.D.** can only be caught by having sexual intercourse with an infected person. If a person has sexual intercourse with many different partners, the chances of becoming infected increase.
3. **GONORRHOEA** and **SYPHILIS** are the two most serious venereal diseases. Gonorrhoea causes sterility, and syphilis damages the nervous system, heart and blood vessels. Both diseases affect men and women.
4. The symptoms of **V.D.** are:
    a. a greenish-yellow discharge from the tip of the penis accompanied by a burning sensation when passing urine, or a yellowish discharge from the vagina;
    b. a raised red spot on the penis or vaginal opening, followed by a brownish rash on the body, sores around the mouth, and a hoarseness of the voice. These symptoms do not necessarily indicate **V.D.** They can be present with other infections.
5. **V.D.** can be treated at special clinics and hospitals.

A satisfactory sexual relationship is not always easy to achieve, and first attempts may leave the sexually inexperienced person feeling disappointed and let down. Enjoyable sexual experiences are often only achieved with much practice. This is more easily obtained with the love, understanding and consideration that comes with a permanent commitment to one partner.

There are other reasons why a sexual relationship should not be entered into lightly. When a girl or young woman makes love, she becomes deeply and emotionally involved. If she is later jilted, she will be hurt far more than if the relationship with her boyfriend had been a friendly, platonic one.

If a young man and young woman love each other and have a stable, caring relationship, the arrival of a baby may be an exciting and longed for event, but babies are not just born to couples who want them. Any sexual relationship resulting in intercourse can lead to a pregnancy. If the couple concerned are young, immature, or just casual friends who do not want to have a permanent relationship, the result may be an unwanted child. Ideally, every child should be wanted and should be able to grow up in the security of a family. Each child needs the love, care and attention of two parents. When a sexual relationship results in an unwanted pregnancy, the couple concerned must decide what to do for the best, bearing in mind their personal feelings for each other, and their moral beliefs. They may ask the advice of their parents, doctor and church. Here are some of the choices open to them. Consider the various solutions and discuss the advantages and disadvantages of each one.

1 They may decide to live together so that the baby can grow up and enjoy a normal family life. Is an unwanted pregnancy a good start for a marriage?

2 The woman may choose to look after the baby herself. As an unmarried mother she will have physical, emotional, social and financial problems to cope with. Discuss these. How is the child of an unmarried mother likely to fare?

3 At birth, the baby may be placed for adoption. This will be a difficult decision for the couple to make. What effect is it likely to have on:

a the unmarried mother;
b the baby;
c the adoptive parents?

4 The mother may decide to have an abortion. Under the 1967 Abortion Act, this is only possible if two registered doctors agree that a continued pregnancy may be harmful to the mother *or* child. Discuss the religious implications of having an abortion.

If an unwanted pregnancy is the result of a casual meeting, the woman may not even know the identity of the father of her child, or he may not be prepared to help her, once she has become pregnant. She may find that she has to deal with her pregnancy alone, without the help and support of her lover. Sometimes, parents find it difficult to excuse what they believe to be immoral behaviour, and will not help a daughter who finds herself "in trouble".

The possibility of an unwanted child is one reason why any young person should consider carefully before entering into a sexual relationship that is not based on deep affection and trust, and it is each individual's responsibility to see that any sexual activity indulged in, does not result in conception.

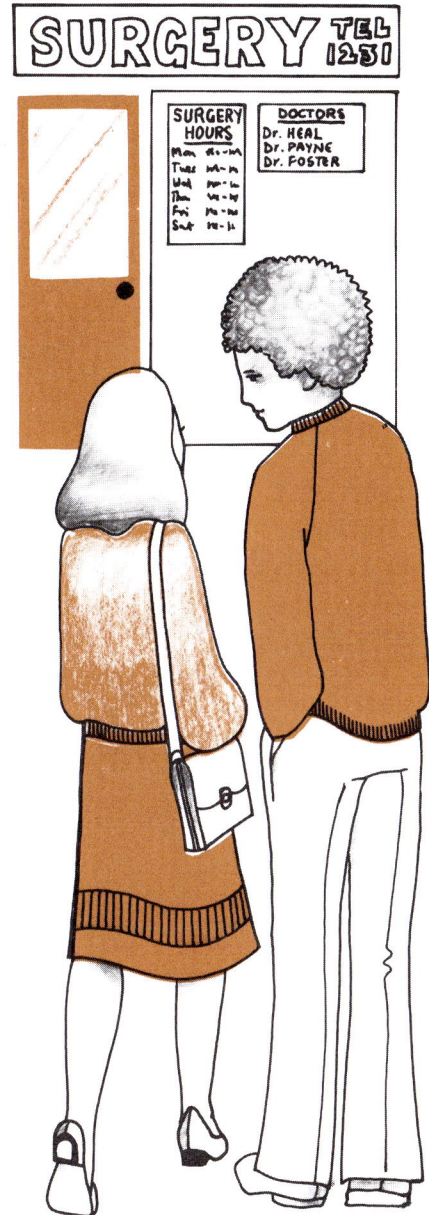

Contraception

Contraception means preventing conception or pregnancy. There are many different methods of contraception available, and the choice of method used will be influenced by a person's:

    a religious beliefs;
    b individual preference;
    c age;
    d existing family.

    Contraception seeks to eliminate the fear of pregnancy, thus allowing a couple to enjoy sexual intercourse to the full. Each method aims at preventing a sperm from fertilizing an ovum. Some methods are more successful and reliable than others. Here are the advantages and disadvantages of each method of contraception. Further information and advice can be obtained from a doctor or local family planning clinic.

The withdrawal method *(Coitus Interruptus)*

With this method the man withdraws his penis from the vagina, before ejaculation.

Advantages	Disadvantages
1 It does not require any preparation, expense or premeditated action.	*1* It is not reliable. Sperm may be released before ejaculation.
2 There is no health risk involved.	*2* This method involves rigid self-control for the man.
	3 It can lead to frustration for both partners.

The "safe period" *(rhythm method)*

This method of contraception involves avoiding intercourse during a period of approximately 10 days around the time of ovulation. The remaining days of the menstrual cycle, from about 10 days before the start of the period until 4 days after its end, are non-fertile days, or the "safe period".

Advantages	*Disadvantages*
1 This method is approved by the Roman Catholic Church. *2* It does not involve any expense. *3* There is no health risk involved.	*1* It is not completely reliable because ovulation can vary from woman to woman, and month to month. *2* A woman who uses this method of contraception must take her temperature each morning so that when it rises she knows an ovum has been released. This can be irksome. *3* This method restricts sexual intercourse to the second half of each menstrual cycle.

The protective sheath *(condom or French letter)*

This consists of a thin, rubber sheath which is worn by the man over his erect penis during intercourse. Semen is trapped in the sheath, which can then be removed and destroyed. A chemical contraceptive cream or jelly should be used by the woman to make this completely reliable.

Advantages	*Disadvantages*
1 This is reliable if properly used. *2* Sheaths can be bought easily from a range of retailers, e.g. chemists, family planning clinics, men's hairdressers. *3* Sheaths offer some protection against V.D. *4* They are hygienic to use. *5* There is no health risk involved. *6* Sheaths can be bought which comply to the British Standards Specification.	*1* A protective sheath has to be unrolled over the erect penis. This involves premeditated action when the man has already become sexually aroused. *2* A sheath can cause a dulling of the sensations. *3* This type of contraceptive has to be bought.

The chemical contraceptive or spermicidal chemical

This consists of a substance which is placed in the vagina to kill the sperm. There are various types available, such as jellies, creams, pessaries and aerosol foams.

Advantages	Disadvantages
1 A chemical contraceptive is easy to use. *2* It can be bought from a range of retailers, e.g. chemists, surgical stores, family planning clinics, mail order companies. *3* It gives lubrication and can be used to prevent chafing when the man is using a protective sheath.	*1* It is less reliable than other forms. *2* It has to be inserted before intercourse. This requires premeditation. *3* This type of contraceptive has to be bought. *4* There is often some distasteful seepage. *5* It may cause irritation.

The diaphragm *(Dutch Cap)*

This method of contraception involves the use of a dome-shaped rubber cup which the woman inserts at the entrance to the uterus. The cap has a spring rim to keep it in position. This diaphragm acts as a barrier and prevents sperm from swimming into the uterus and Fallopian tubes.

Advantages	Disadvantages
1 This is a reliable form of contraceptive, if used **with** a chemical spermicide. *2* There is no health risk involved. *3* The diaphragm cannot be felt during intercourse nor does it dull the sensations.	*1* The diaphragm can be obtained from a doctor or family planning clinic, who must check that the correct size is used, and also give the woman instructions on how to insert and remove it herself. This can prove distasteful. *2* The diaphragm has to be inserted before intercourse. This involves premeditation. *3* The cap must be left in position for 6 to 8 hours after intercourse, then removed and cleansed. *4* Check-ups are needed periodically to ensure that the cap is fitting snugly. *5* If a cap has not been fitted correctly it will be uncomfortable to wear, and unreliable.

An intra-uterine device *(coil or loop)*

An I.U.D. is a small plastic or copper-coated ring or coil which is inserted inside the uterus. It aims to prevent a fertilized ovum from attaching itself to the uterine wall.

Advantages	Disadvantages
1 Once the I.U.D. has been fitted by a doctor, no other form of contraceptive is necessary.	*1* The initial fitting of an I.U.D. may be painful, especially for a woman who has not had a baby.
2 It is a reliable form of contraception.	*2* It can cause heavy periods and cramp pains.
3 The I.U.D. cannot be felt during intercourse, nor does it dull the sensations.	*3* An I.U.D. can sometimes be expelled from the body naturally. If this is not noticed, pregnancy may occur.
4 An ordinary plastic I.U.D. can be left in the uterus indefinitely (but see disadvantages point 4).	*4* A copper I.U.D. must be replaced every 2 years.

The oral contraceptive or "pill"

The oral contraceptive is a hormonal tablet which is swallowed by the woman. It prevents ovulation and changes the lining of the cervix making it difficult for sperm to enter the uterus. There are several types of "pill" and they each can have a high or low dose of oestrogen.

Advantages	Disadvantages
1 This is a reliable method of contraception.	*1* There **are** health hazards. The risk of dying from heart attacks and strokes increases with the "pill". The women most at risk are those who: *a* are over 35; *b* have been taking the "pill" continuously for over 5 years; *c* smoke.
2 It is easy to use.	
3 Once the tablet has been swallowed, no other form of contraceptive is necessary. Intercourse may be had without any further preparation or precaution.	*2* The "pill" can have unpleasant side effects, such as headaches, weight gain, depression and sickness.
4 The "pill" can be readily obtained from a chemist or family planning clinic, but a doctor's prescription is required.	*3* A medical examination is necessary because it is not suited to all women.
	4 A regular blood pressure check is advisable.

Sterilization

This is a surgical operation aimed at preventing pregnancy. It may be performed on a man or woman.

Male sterilization is called **vasectomy** and consists of cutting and tying the tubes which carry the sperm from the testicles to the penis. This means that intercourse can take place normally, but no sperm will be present in the semen.

Advantages	Disadvantage
1 This is a simple operation.	This operation is generally permanent. A reversal operation is rarely successful. This means that a man who decides to have a vasectomy should:
2 It is completely reliable as a means of contraception, but additional methods should be used for the first six months after the operation.	*a* be certain that he and his partner will not want another baby in the future;
3 After six months, intercourse may be had without any further preparation or precautions.	*b* be content with his existing partner. (A separation, divorce and remarriage could mean that a man would be unable to father children again with a new partner.)
4 There is no health risk involved.	

Female sterilization is called **tubal ligation** and is a more complex operation than vasectomy, because the Fallopian tubes, which need to be cut and tied, are not near the surface of the abdomen.

Advantages	Disadvantages
1 It is completely reliable as a means of contraception.	*1* Modern techniques have helped to simplify this operation but it is still easier if carried out immediately after childbirth, when the Fallopian tubes are nearer to the surface.
2 It is effective immediately. Intercourse may be had without any further preparation or precaution.	*2* This operation is generally permanent. A reversal operation is rarely successful.

A man or woman considering sterilization should seek professional advice and counselling, and should be fully aware of the long-term implications of the operation. Surgeons are reluctant to sterilize young people unless there are medical reasons for doing so.

Starting a family

A human baby is a helpless individual which has to be sheltered, fed, clothed and cared for during its early years. At birth it is entirely dependent on other people, and for survival relies on the type of care it receives during infancy. Because a human baby is so helpless it needs the love, care and attention of two parents, who will share the responsibility for its upbringing. The family system evolved to give security to the young. It allows a baby to grow up in comfortable surroundings, with a happy mother-father-child relationship. A secure family background is vital to the developing child, who needs constant love, sympathy, encouragement, tolerance, understanding and respect from those around him.

The family unit usually grows out of the union of a man and woman who are married. Marriage is a contract which can be entered into during a legal or religious ceremony. During the marriage ceremony, a man and woman announce their love for each other and their intention of living together. Their union is blessed by the church, and approved by society which acknowledges that any offspring of the marriage will be legitimate. Some couples choose to live together as man and wife but reject the idea of marriage, and for others marriage would be illegal because of an existing spouse.

It used to be a fact of life that the birth of a baby was an inevitable result of sexual intercourse, but effective contraception now means that couples can decide whether, and when, to start a family. They can, if they wish, delay having a baby until they feel financially secure and able to provide for their offspring. A woman can now carry on with a career, even after marriage, and can look forward to a healthier life, having been freed from the debilitating (weakening) effects of repeated pregnancies.

The children which are now conceived should be "wanted" children, and should be able to grow up healthier and happier because their arrival was planned.

Think and Do

1. What are the dangers involved in casual sexual relationships?

2. In your notebook, write a paragraph on each of the following:
a. the marriage ceremony;
b. the religious aspects involved in planning a family;
c. sterilization.

3. Why is a secure family background important to a young child?

4. Why is it unwise for a young girl to try to sexually arouse her boyfriend?

5. What advice would you offer an unmarried mother-to-be? Where could she go for help?

6. Copy the following diagram into your notebook. Write a suitable sentence in each of the boxes.

METHODS OF CONTRACEPTION

COITUS INTERRUPTUS	CHEMICAL CONTRACEPTIVES	THE SHEATH	THE 'SAFE PERIOD'

THE DIAPHRAGM	STERILIZATION	ORAL CONTRACEPTIVES	INTRA-UTERINE DEVICES

7. Find out where you would go and what you would do to:
a. obtain contraceptive advice;
b. receive treatment for a venereal disease;
c. arrange to have an unborn baby adopted;
d. get financial help from the state for an unmarried mother who wishes to keep her baby;
e. register a marriage.

8. Copy the following sentences into your notebook. Say whether each one is *true* or *false*.
a. V.D. can only be caught by having sexual intercourse with an infected person.
b. A copper I.U.D. can be left in the uterus indefinitely.
c. The rhythm method of contraception is approved by the Roman Catholic Church.
d. Sterilization can be reversed by a simple operation.
e. It is not advisable for a woman who is over 35, has been taking the "pill" for longer than 5 years and smokes, to use the oral contraceptive.

9. Visit your school and local libraries and find out all you can about Marie Stopes and her work on family planning.

10. Copy out this crossword and complete it.

Clues across
1. Male sterilization.
2. This method of contraception confines sexual intercourse to the "safe period" in each menstrual cycle.
3. The oral contraceptive.

Clues down
4. Also called the "French letter".
5. An I.U.D.
6. A venereal disease.

Pregnancy

When a woman has had intercourse, especially during ovulation (her fertile part of the month), she may start looking for signs of pregnancy.

Signs of pregnancy

The first sign of a suspected pregnancy is a missed monthly period. If menstruation has been regular, and an expected period is more than 10 days late, it is likely that conception has occurred.

A missed period, though, does not always mean that a woman is pregnant. Tensions and emotional upsets can sometimes cause a temporary break in a normal monthly cycle.

Other signs and symptoms of pregnancy are:

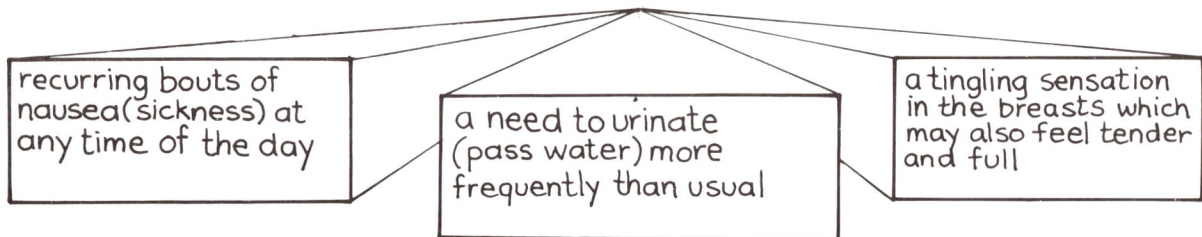

recurring bouts of nausea (sickness) at any time of the day

a need to urinate (pass water) more frequently than usual

a tingling sensation in the breasts which may also feel tender and full

When pregnancy is suspected it is wise for a woman to visit her doctor as soon as possible. If it is a first pregnancy, she may want to ask questions and be reassured about secret worries. If the pregnancy is into the third month (two periods having been missed), a doctor will be able to confirm pregnancy by a clinical examination. At this stage the enlarging uterus can be felt through the abdomen wall. Sometimes it is necessary to have an earlier confirmation of pregnancy, and this can be done by testing a woman's urine for excessive amounts of hormone. The result of the test will be either positive, thus confirming pregnancy, or negative.

Ante-natal care

Ante-natal care refers to the medical help and supervision given to an expectant mother prior to the birth of her baby. Many specially trained people are available to help the mother have a trouble-free pregnancy, and to keep a check on her baby's growth and health.

The importance of regular visits to the doctor or clinic

When pregnancy is confirmed, a doctor will carry out a general routine examination, and ask questions about the expectant mother's medical history and that of her family. Arrangements will be made for regular routine checks, either with her doctor or at a convenient ante-natal clinic, so that the health of both the mother and baby can be watched throughout the pregnancy. These visits are usually arranged once a month until the final weeks of pregnancy, when routine checks become fortnightly and then weekly.

At each of these visits, the mother will be examined for:

a. excessive weight increase;

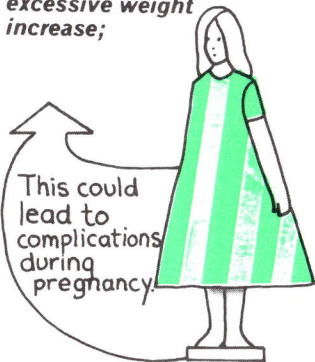

This could lead to complications during pregnancy.

b. raised blood pressure;

If untreated this would be very dangerous for the baby.

c. the presence of sugar or albumen in her urine.

These could indicate diabetes, kidney or bladder infections or developing toxaemia (a poisoning of the blood).

She may also be given a vaginal examination during which the doctor feels for any abnormalities which may cause problems at the birth of the baby. A "smear" test for cervical cancer will be taken during the internal examination.

Regular checks are essential to the health and well-being of both the mother and baby. Disorders and illnesses can be discovered quickly, and prompt treatment given, and any worries or fears can be "talked out" with the doctor. Regular visits allow the mother to build up a relationship with the trained staff who will help at the birth of her baby, and this gives confidence to the expectant mother who may feel unsure and bewildered. Advice is available on various health aspects, such as diet, exercise, choosing comfortable clothing and dealing with the minor physical discomforts of pregnancy.

Blood tests

A specimen of blood will be taken during the first ante-natal examination. This is usually withdrawn from the arm of the mother. It is used to determine the blood group that would be required in the event of a transfusion. There are 4 different blood groups: A; B; AB and O. Group O is the most common. A blood test will also determine whether the mother is anaemic. She may require extra iron, which can be prescribed in tablet form or as capsules.

Red blood cells contain a feature called the **rhesus factor** which may be either positive (Rh +) or negative (Rh −). If the blood of an expectant mother is found to be Rh −, extra care will be taken during her pregnancy. There is little danger of complications during a first pregnancy, but succeeding babies may be at risk, if the mother has developed substances called **antibodies** in her blood.

Rh disease can be prevented by testing the blood of Rh − mothers, after the birth of their first baby, to see if antibodies have been formed. If antibodies are present in the mother's blood, then treatment can be given which will destroy the antibodies so that subsequent pregnancies are not threatened. Where Rh disease is found to be present in a new-born baby, the blood can be exchanged by transfusion, and Rh − blood used to replace the Rh + blood.

Detecting abnormalities in the unborn baby

Most babies are born perfectly formed and healthy but a small proportion of all live births are abnormal. The reasons for some of these abnormalities are not fully understood, but many can be traced to:

a hereditary factors;
b damage to the foetus during pregnancy and birth.

When a child is born with an inherited disorder, parents are advised to consult a geneticist to determine whether any children they may have in the future are likely to inherit the same abnormality. They must then decide whether they wish to have another baby. Some abnormalities, such as *spina bifida* (a condition where part of the spinal cord is exposed) and *mongolism*, can be detected in the unborn child. The parents are then given the option of terminating the pregnancy or having a child that is going to be handicapped for life.

The Abortion Act of 1967 states that a pregnancy may be terminated if two registered medical practitioners agree that:

a the continued pregnancy would involve a risk to the life of the woman or injure her physical or mental health, or that of her existing family;

b there would be a risk that the child would be born suffering from such a degree of physical or mental subnormality that it would be seriously handicapped.

A simple blood test can indicate whether a pregnant woman is likely to give birth to a baby with spina bifida. If the blood test shows a high level of A.F.P. (alpha-fetoprotein) in the mother's blood, then the presence of spina bifida is likely. *Amniocentesis* is a test which involves inserting a needle into the uterus and drawing off some amniotic fluid for testing. This method of detecting abnormalities can be used for spina bifida, mongolism and other defects in unborn babies.

Expectant mothers over 40 years of age are more likely to give birth to abnormal babies than younger mothers, and for this reason they are often advised to undergo special screening tests.

Some abnormalities can be traced back to pregnancy during which the developing foetus was damaged. Thalidomide was a drug which had passed the normal safety tests and was marketed in 1957. Doctors prescribed it as a sedative. Evidence slowly began to accumulate linking Thalidomide with a sharp rise in the number of babies who were being born with deformed arms and legs. The mothers of these babies had taken the drug during the early stages of pregnancy. The Thalidomide tragedy shows clearly how a developing foetus can be damaged by drugs. Damage can also be caused by:

1 German measles. If an expectant mother is in contact with German measles during the first four months of pregnancy, she should see her doctor who will be able to give treatment, if necessary. It is wise preventive medicine to immunize young girls against German measles *before* the possibility of pregnancy.

2 Smoking. Tests have shown that babies born to "smoking" mothers have cyanide compounds in their urine. They are smaller than average at birth and may be less intelligent than children from mothers who do not smoke. This could be due to the fact that they have not developed to their full potential before birth.

Danger signals during pregnancy

Occasionally during pregnancy there may be warning signs that all is not well. If a mother feels ill or has some unusual and unexpected symptoms, she should seek her doctor's advice immediately. An expectant mother should never ignore any:

aches, stabbing pains or contractions in the abdomen

bleeding, heavy discharge or rush of water from the vagina

Dr. E. Speck

loss or blurring of vision and persistent or feverish headaches

signs of swelling to the face, hands, ankles or legs

If she is unlucky and has a bad fall, then an expectant mother should go straight to bed and send for her doctor. Miscarriages can be caused by hard falls, especially in early pregnancy.

As soon as pregnancy is confirmed, it is essential that a doctor should know if a woman:

    a has diabetes;
    b may have a venereal disease;
    c has had rheumatic fever;
    d suffers from a congenital heart disorder;
    e has had tuberculosis.

Preparing for childbirth

An expectant mother, especially in her first pregnancy, will want to learn all she can about her unborn baby. She will want to know exactly what will happen during labour and how she can help her baby at its birth. A sensible mother will read all she can about the subject, and will join one of the many ante-natal classes available. These classes set out to offer instruction on childbirth, so that the mother understands what is happening to her body and to her baby during labour (see chapter 6). The importance of relaxation is stressed and exercises are practised to help the mother to relax between contractions (the rhythmic movements of the muscles in childbirth). She may also be advised on breathing techniques that will help to control the contractions during labour. These courses often cater for both parents, and the father-to-be is encouraged to help during pregnancy and labour, so that the birth of their baby can be a shared event. He will be shown how to help with breathing and relaxation exercises, and how to encourage, support and comfort the mother during the delivery. Many fathers wish to be present at the birth so that they can share in their baby's first moments, and some maternity units and midwives will welcome this.

The idea of "natural childbirth" was publicized by the late Dr Grantly Dick Read, who felt strongly that fear and ignorance combined to make childbirth a more painful experience than was necessary. He taught that an understanding of the various stages of labour helped a mother to

control her contractions, and to co-operate during delivery, thus allowing her to enjoy the birth.

Ante-natal classes can also offer instruction on baby care and parentcraft. Fathers are encouraged to play their part here too, so that having a baby and caring for it becomes a shared experience. Films and slides may be shown and there is plenty of opportunity for new parents-to-be to ask questions and seek advice.

Diet during pregnancy

It is important for an expectant mother to eat a well-planned and varied diet, so that her body and her baby will receive all the nutrients necessary for healthy growth. The baby will take all its requirements from the mother's body, and if she is not eating sensibly to replace this loss, her own health will suffer. She may quickly become deficient in calcium, iron and vitamins. During pregnancy, a mother's daily diet should contain a good supply of:

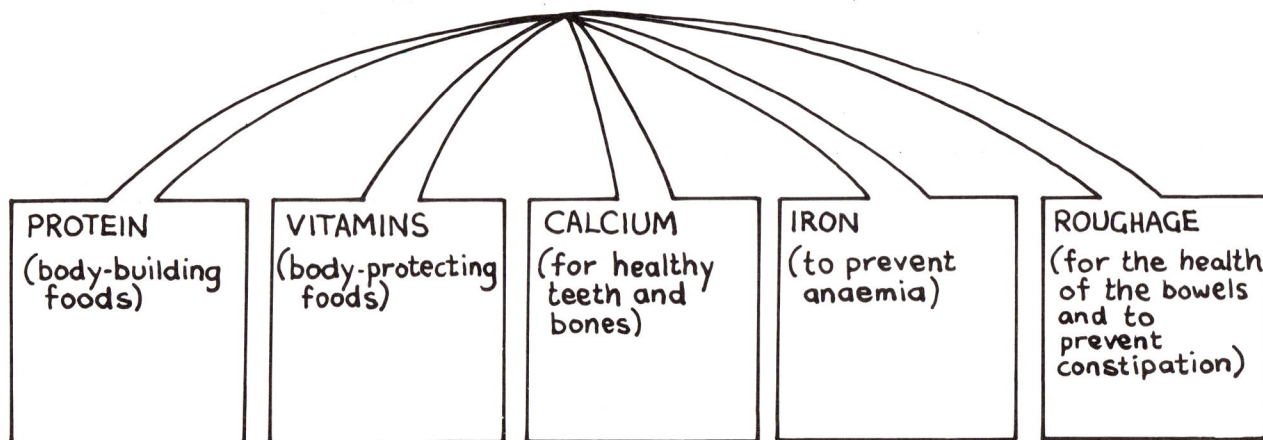

PROTEIN (body-building foods)	VITAMINS (body-protecting foods)	CALCIUM (for healthy teeth and bones)	IRON (to prevent anaemia)	ROUGHAGE (for the health of the bowels and to prevent constipation)

The chart opposite shows some good sources of nutrients.

A sensible, varied diet will ensure that an expectant mother obtains all the nutrients that her body and her baby need. A doctor may prescribe iron and vitamin tablets which should be taken in addition to a normal balanced diet.

Nutrient	Where found
Protein	All meat, fish, eggs, milk, cheese, pulse vegetables (peas, beans, lentils), nuts
Vitamins A	Liver, kidney, oily fish, fats, cheese, carrots
B complex	Liver, whole cereals, yeast, milk, nuts, root, pulse and leafy vegetables
C	Citrus fruits, raw vegetables, fresh fruits, potatoes
D	Fats, oily fish, egg yolk, sunlight on the skin
E	Vegetable fats, egg yolk, dairy produce, wholemeal bread
K	Leafy vegetables
Calcium	Milk, cheese, bread, nuts, oily fish (especially sardines, pilchards, salmon), green vegetables, egg yolk
Iron	Egg yolk, liver, kidney, dried fruits (especially prunes, raisins, peaches), leafy green vegetables (especially spinach, parsley, sprouts)
Roughage dietary fibre	Wholemeal bread, porridge, fresh fruit, green vegetables, natural bran

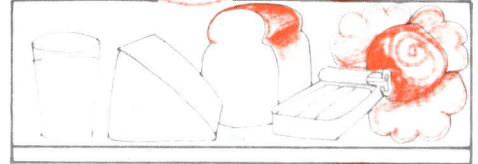

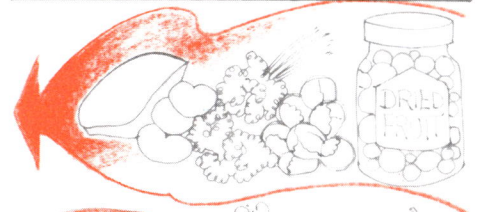

During pregnancy, a woman should avoid *large* amounts of:

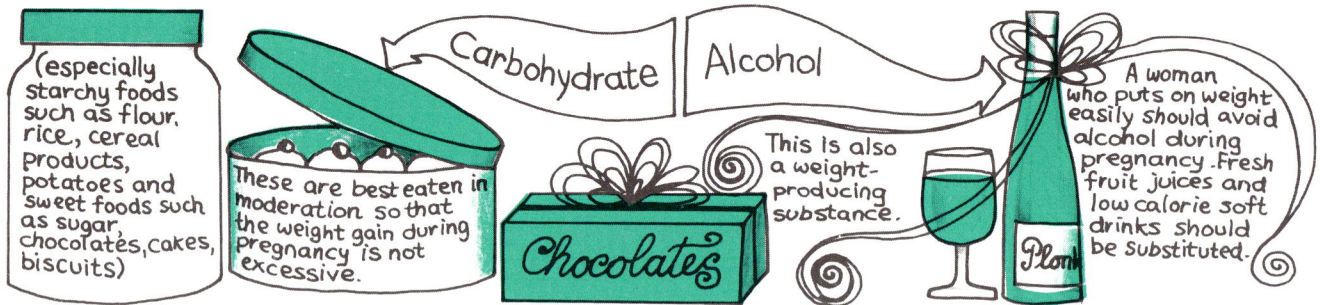

(especially starchy foods such as flour, rice, cereal products, potatoes and sweet foods such as sugar, chocolates, cakes, biscuits)

These are best eaten in moderation so that the weight gain during pregnancy is not excessive.

Carbohydrate

Alcohol

Chocolates

This is also a weight-producing substance.

A woman who puts on weight easily should avoid alcohol during pregnancy. Fresh fruit juices and low calorie soft drinks should be substituted.

Plonk

Excessive weight gain during pregnancy is harmful because it is:

a damaging to the mother's health;
b likely to cause complications in the pregnancy;
c difficult to lose after the birth of the baby.

Health during pregnancy

During a normal pregnancy an expectant mother will often feel exceptionally healthy. She may feel more energetic than usual and want to indulge in plenty of fresh air and exercise. This can only prove beneficial to her and the baby, so long as she remembers not to:

a overtire herself;
b take part in strenuous exercise that involves jumping, lifting or straining.

WEIGH-U

Some suitable exercises and activities.

dancing

walking

riding

playing "gentle" games of tennis

swimming

An expectant mother should get plenty of rest. At least 8 hours sleep at night is recommended, with a rest during the daytime, preferably with the legs in a raised position.

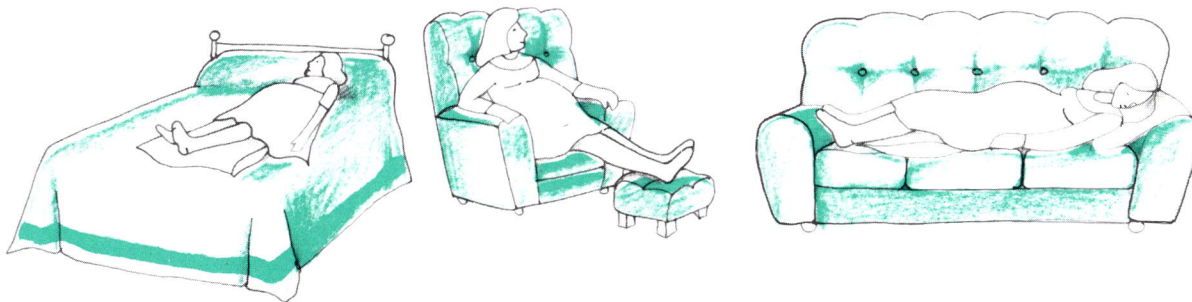

A daily bath or shower is advisable during pregnancy. It is especially important to cleanse and freshen between the legs, because an expectant mother may have a slight vaginal discharge from time to time. (It is **not normal** for a discharge to be heavy or thick. This is a sign that all is not well and a doctor should be notified.)

In addition to these basic rules of health, a pregnant woman should:

visit her dentist to check that her teeth are in good condition

refrain from taking drugs or medicines which have not been specifically prescribed for HER

eat a regular supply of "bulky" foods, so that she does not become constipated

avoid close contact with people who are suffering from infectious diseases, heavy colds and 'flu

have a natural posture, holding herself erect

eat a well-balanced diet

visit her doctor or ante-natal clinic for regular, routine checks

be careful not to put on too much weight

dress attractively

give up smoking

Choosing clothes during pregnancy

During pregnancy, clothes should be attractive and comfortable to wear. They should not constrict the body, or pull tightly across the bust, waist or legs. Loosely-falling, stylish garments are ideal.

Foundation garments should be the correct size, so that the body is supported gently without being "pulled-in". It is important that the breasts are not flattened during pregnancy. An adjustable bra that has a front fastening, will prove useful when breast-feeding. The stomach should be supported from below by a lightweight maternity girdle, or pair of stretch maternity pantees. Maternity corsets may be needed in subsequent pregnancies, if the stomach muscles have become stretched and flabby.

Shoes should have a low heel, be strong enough to support the extra body weight, and wide enough to fit the feet comfortably.

The development of the foetus during a normal pregnancy

In chapter 2 we learned about conception and we discovered that by the end of the second month of pregnancy a foetus has begun to resemble a human baby, having developed head, face, legs and arms. It is still incredibly small and measures about 1 cm in length.

During the next month, nails appear on the fingers and toes, and eyelids develop but remain tightly fused together. By the end of the third month the foetus measures about 2 cm in length and weighs about 28 g. The mother's abdomen has begun to grow to accommodate the enlarging uterus, and she will notice a thickening of the waist and a tightness across the hips, when wearing her normal clothes.

It is during the fourth or fifth month that a mother will start to feel her baby move. This is called "quickening", and the foetus may kick out violently and thrash its arms, as it twists and turns in the amniotic sac. Its vital organs are formed and functioning. The head, which is large in proportion to the rest of the body, now has hair, and by the end of the fifth month the baby's heartbeat can be clearly heard by a doctor. It now weighs around 450 g.

During the sixth month of pregnancy the baby grows in length to about 30 cm, and eyelashes and eyebrows appear.

By the end of the seventh month the baby's skin looks red and wrinkled. It can now open its eyes, and weighs around 1·5 kg. During the eighth and ninth months the baby grows fatter and its skin becomes paler. By the end of the pregnancy it will weigh approximately 3·25 kg and be around 50 cm in length. It spends the final days of pregnancy in a curled position with its head downwards against the cervix, waiting to be born.

During pregnancy the uterus swells in size until it reaches the bottom of the mother's ribs and it protrudes at the front of the abdomen.

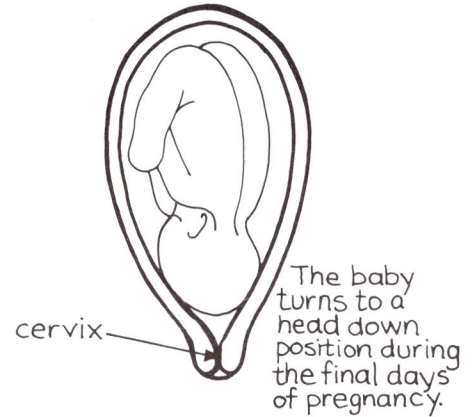

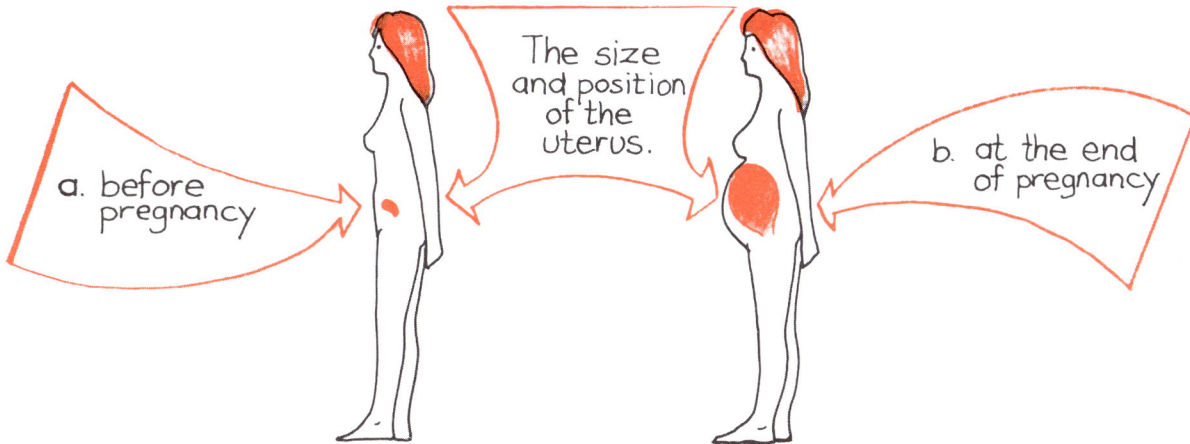

cervix

The baby turns to a head down position during the final days of pregnancy.

The size and position of the uterus.

a. before pregnancy

b. at the end of pregnancy

Think and Do

1. Why should an expectant mother consider her diet carefully? List some foods which are good sources of calcium and iron. What foods should be avoided during pregnancy?

2. How can a father help:

a. during pregnancy;

b. at the birth of the baby?

3. Why is it important for a pregnant woman to visit her doctor regularly? Describe two of the tests that are usually carried out at an ante-natal check-up.

4. In your notebook, list the ways in which an unborn child can be harmed by its mother.

5. Explain what is meant by the following terms:

a. quickening;

b. natural childbirth;

c. amniocentesis.

6. What important information can be obtained from a blood test during pregnancy?

7. List the maternity clothes you would advise an expectant mother to buy. What points should be considered when choosing:

a. foundation garments;

b. footwear?

8. What do you understand by the term "Rhesus factor"? How can a mother with Rh− blood be helped during pregnancy and after the birth?

9. Copy the following sentences into your notebook. Say whether each one is *true* or *false*.

a. It is not wise for a pregnant woman to increase her weight excessively.

b. Roughage in the diet helps to prevent anaemia.

c. A smear test is for cervical cancer.

d. Expectant mothers over the age of forty are more likely to give birth to abnormal babies than younger mothers.

e. High blood pressure can damage an unborn baby.

f. Group AB is the most common of the blood groups.

10. How can an expectant mother remain fit and healthy during pregnancy?

Preparing for the birth

With the introduction of modern methods of contraception, most pregnancies should be planned. When a baby is planned or wanted, pregnancy becomes a very special and exciting time. Both parents-to-be look forward to the birth of their baby with a relaxed, happy frame of mind. They obtain much pleasure from choosing nursery equipment, collecting a layette and preparing for the birth of their baby.

Claiming maternity benefits
Maternity benefits are available to help towards the cost of having a baby. An expectant mother is entitled to claim a *maternity grant*. The maternity grant can be claimed at any time from nine weeks before the birth, to three months after the baby is born.

If an expectant mother is working and paying a full national insurance contribution, she will be entitled to a *maternity allowance*, in addition to the grant. This is a weekly payment which lasts for eighteen weeks. The first allowance is paid eleven weeks before the expected birth.

A leaflet (NI 17A), which can be obtained from a Social Security office, explains all about maternity benefits.

Free vitamins, prescriptions, dental treatment, glasses and milk tokens are also available for the expectant mother. A leaflet (MI 1), available at Post Offices, explains who is eligible.

An expectant mother who already has a family, may be entitled to claim free school dinners for her existing children. Details of this family benefit can be obtained from the local Education office (local District Welfare office in Scotland).

A doctor must confirm pregnancy before any of these maternity benefits are available.

Choosing nursery equipment
Buying nursery equipment is expensive but some sensible economies can be made. The large items of furniture, such

as a pram, cot, pushchair, playpen and high chair may be:

1 bought from a shop or department which specializes in nursery equipment;

2 bought second-hand from friends, or in answer to "for sale" notices in newspapers or newsagents' windows;

3 loaned or handed down from one member of a family to another.

Equipping the nursery, therefore, need not turn out to be as expensive as first feared.

Here are some points to consider when choosing a pram.

1 A pram with a soft body is light and convenient to handle, but a metal-bodied pram will last longer.

2 A detachable body with a collapsing chassis is convenient when travelling in a car. Always check that the two parts are easy to detach and handle. The mechanism that is used to collapse the chassis should be childproof.

3 A good pram should be stable and not easy to tip over. A shopping tray which fixes across the wheels gives more stability than a basket/shopping bag which is attached to the handle of the pram.

4 The internal surface of the pram should be roomy, comfortable and well padded. Look for ease of cleaning and avoid prams with awkward corners, rims and ledges. There should be no sharp features which could hurt a child.

5 The brake should be out of a child's reach, and should operate on at least two of the wheels.

6 A pram with a detachable body should have strong, securely attached carrying handles which are easy to hold.

7 A pram should be well sprung. Springs which operate on front **and** back wheels give a smoother ride.

8 Check that the pram will go through your door easily.

9 Small wheels can give an uncomfortably bumpy ride. Large wheels give a smoother ride but can be bulky to handle. A pram with one set of large and one set of small wheels is both comfortable and easy to manoeuvre up and down kerbstones.

10 Harness rings should be low down and securely attached to the body of the pram. Rings which are too high allow a baby to turn a somersault whilst in the harness and are potentially dangerous.

11 It is sensible to look for a good make and, if possible, buy from a reputable firm. Many retailers will store a pram until the baby is born and will agree to keep an ordered pram in the event of a miscarriage or stillbirth.

Here are some points to consider when choosing a pushchair.

1 A pushchair should be sturdy and well made.

2 There should be no sharp features which could hurt a child.

3 Harness rings should be low down and securely attached to the body of the pushchair.

4 The brake should be out of a toddler's reach, and should operate on at least two of the wheels.

5 It should be stable and not easily tipped over. If a shopping tray/basket is provided, it should fit low down on the pushchair. This lowers the centre of gravity and gives more stability.

6 The mechanism that is used to collapse the pushchair should be childproof. This should be examined carefully. Fatalities and bad accidents have been caused by pushchairs which have collapsed on to the occupant, trapping head, arms or legs. British manufacturers and retailers insist on a high standard of safety in their nursery goods, but *do check*.

7 It is sensible to look for a good make of pushchair and, if possible, buy from a reputable firm.

A new-born baby can sleep in a:

   a carrycot;
   b crib;
   c detachable body of a folding pram;
   d full-sized cot.

If a carrycot is used it should be placed on a strong and stable stand that will not tip over. Similarly, a crib should stand firm and secure. A miniature cot on rockers is not a good idea because it can easily be pulled over by an eager toddler climbing up to see his new baby brother or sister. If a pram body is used as a baby's first bed, it should be left on the securely braked chassis, if at all possible. Where stairs have to be negotiated, the pram body should be detached and then body and chassis carried upstairs separately, to be reassembled in the bedroom. If the chassis

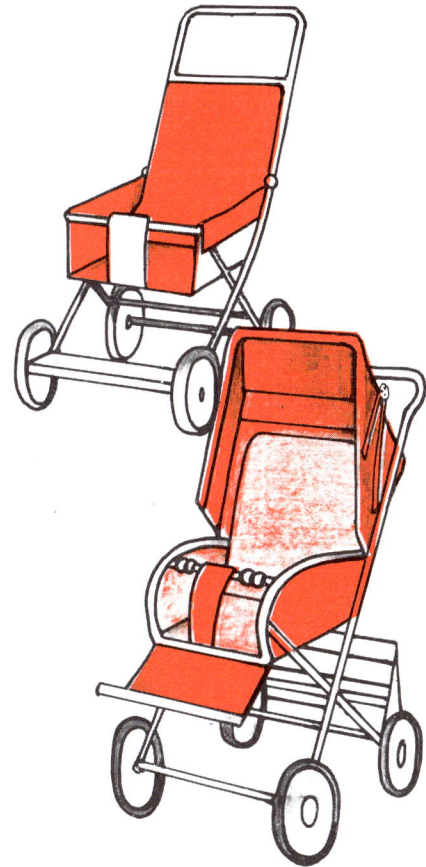

is too bulky for this, the detached pram body should be positioned on a flat surface where it cannot tip over. It is unwise to rest a pram body (or carrycot) on a spare bed, especially if there are lively toddlers or active pets in the home. After the first few weeks, a baby should sleep in a cot during the night.

Here are some points to consider when choosing a cot.

1 The space between the bars of a cot should measure 75 mm to 100 mm. If the space is smaller, a baby may trap its arms or legs. If the space is larger, the baby's head may get caught between the bars.

2 It is a good idea to choose a cot whose mattress can be lowered when a baby becomes more active. The space between the bottom of the bars and the base of the cot should be narrower than the thickness of the mattress.

3 Plastic-coated nursery transfers, which could peel off easily and be swallowed, are not a good idea for the inside surfaces of a cot.

4 Some cots convert into first-size beds when the sides are removed.

5 If a second-hand cot is bought which needs to be re-decorated, it is essential that a *lead-free* paint is used. A baby, when teething, will gnaw at any surface and can be poisoned by a toxic paint.

6 A cot will usually have one side that will drop down. This makes it easier to lower the baby on to the mattress without straining over the side of the cot. The mechanism for adjusting the drop side should be childproof, with no sharp edges that could harm the baby.

7 A cot mattress should be firm so that a baby will not sink into it and suffocate. An interior sprung or foam-filled mattress is suitable. The mattress should have a smooth, waterproof covering that can be wiped clean. Buttons, which can be swallowed, and quilted stitching, which can be unpicked, should be avoided. The plastic protective bag on a new mattress *must* be removed before use. This could be sucked into a baby's mouth, causing asphyxiation.

8 Drawers on castors, which can be stored under a cot, can provide valuable storage space for clothes, toys and nursery equipment.

A baby will require a selection of bedding. This must range in size to fit the type of nursery equipment used, e.g. smaller items which are suitable for a carrycot, crib or pushchair, and larger sized bedding for prams and cots. A good supply of bedding is important, so that there are always enough clean, well-aired sheets and blankets to cope with any emergency. It is often possible to make sensible economies by hemming around the best parts of old full-sized sheets and blankets. Bedding which is bought by the metre, and hemmed on a sewing machine, can also save pennies. A new double-sized blanket or sheet can be cut down and hemmed to make four cot-sized items, with possibly a couple of smaller pieces left which could be used in a crib, carrycot or pushchair. With a little thought and planning, therefore, accumulating a good supply of baby bedding need not be too expensive.

Here are some points to consider when choosing bedding for a baby.

1 A baby under 12 months old should ***not*** sleep on a pillow. When choosing a pillow for an older baby, look for a washable pillow that is firm to the touch. It should be completely porous, so that vomit can drain through easily. A pillowcase should be washable and of an open weave through which a baby can breathe. A cotton or stretch towelling pillowcase is suitable.

2 Man-made fabrics are easy to launder but are not absorbent. Polyester/cotton and cotton/nylon mixtures give the comfort and absorbency of cotton combined with the washable, non-iron properties of man-made fabrics. Stretch towelling sheets are very absorbent, comfortable and easy to wash. Fitted sheets with mitred corners give a wrinkle-free surface and are easily slipped on and off the mattress.

3 A small, waterproof sheet will give extra protection to the bedding in a pram or cot. It should be placed under the bottom sheet. Some waterproof sheets have one side covered in a fleecy towelling fabric which is warm and comfortable for the baby.

4 A continental quilt can be used on a pram or cot. This gives freedom of movement to a baby. It is light in weight

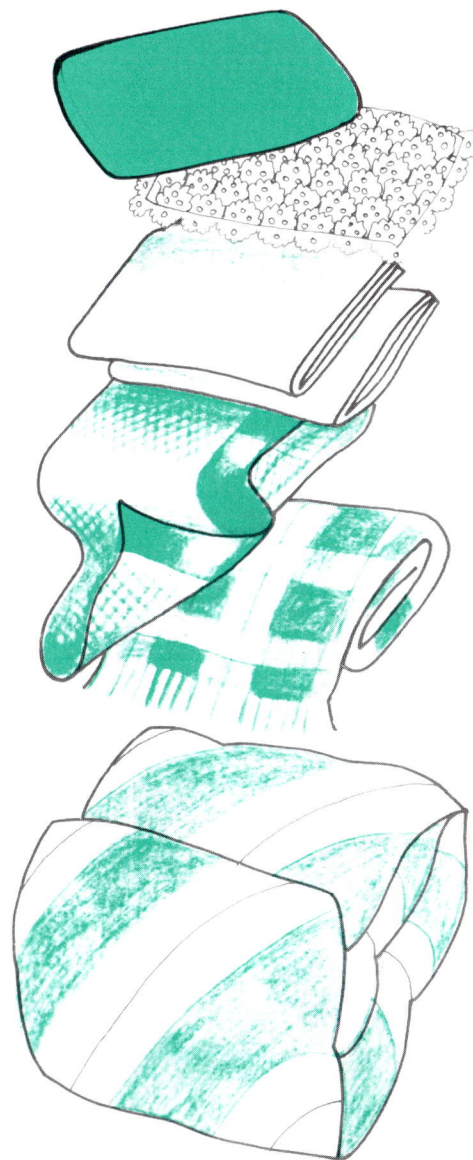

but warm and cosy. A machine-washable continental quilt should be chosen. Covers should be warm to the touch but easily washed. A cotton/man-made mixture fabric is suitable.

5 Cellular blankets are the safest kind because they allow a baby to breathe easily, even if the blankets are pulled over his face. Cellular cotton blankets can be boiled, but they do shrink and take longer to dry than man-made fabrics. Cellular acrylic blankets are ideal. Baby blankets should be lightweight so that they do not restrict movement. They should be wide enough to be tucked under the mattress at either side. Bound or hemmed edges are preferable to fringed ends. An older baby can pull at fringing and swallow loose threads.

There are other items of furniture which will be needed in a nursery.

1 Storage space will be needed for baby equipment, clothes and toys. A large, old-fashioned chest of drawers can be redecorated to give valuable storage space. Old trunks and tea-chests can be gaily decorated and used for storing toys. Special nursery furniture units can be bought that combine a child's wardrobe with a set of drawers and a storage cupboard.

2 A nursery will need a source of heat, for use in cold weather. If a separate heater is used, it should be placed out of a young child's reach or be protected by a sturdy guard. A convector heater or storage heater will give adequate warmth without drying up the atmosphere, but remember that all metal surfaces of the heater will get **hot**. A central heating radiator is useful because baby clothes can be safely draped over it for airing purposes.

3 The floor surface should be easy to clean. A patterned or cushioned vinyl, or a linoleum floor covering can be washed down. Carpet tiles can be scrubbed clean and turned to hide obstinate stains. A bonded or man-made fibre carpet can be sponged down. Washable scatter rugs with a non-slip backing can add warmth and colour.

Equipment will also be needed for bathing and changing the baby.

1 If the bathroom is cold, it is better to bath a baby in the nursery. An ordinary rigid plastic baby bath is suitable. This can be placed on the floor, or on a secure bathstand. A baby bath which has a sloping bottom surface is a good idea. This allows the baby to lie comfortably in the bath with his head out of the water. A baby should **never** be left alone in a bath.

2 A bag, tray, cardboard box or basket should be available with all the toiletries that will be needed when bathing, changing and feeding the baby. These will be useful:

- *a* a box of paper tissues, a roll of kitchen paper or a roll of soft, absorbent toilet paper;
- *b* cotton wool;
- *c* cotton swabs for cleaning the nose and ears;
- *d* a baby brush and comb;
- *e* small nail scissors;
- *f* baby soap, powder, shampoo and lotion;
- *g* zinc and castor oil cream or Vaseline petroleum jelly;
- *h* nappy pins.

It is helpful to remember that savings can be made by buying large or giant-sized toiletries. A special liquid, soapless bath oil can be used instead of soap. This can also be used as a shampoo.

A baby will also require other items of furniture which can be moved around the house as required.

1 A high chair with a detachable feeding tray makes meal times easier. Look for a sturdy chair that has a washable surface and a comfortably padded seat. When redecorating wooden chairs, use a non-toxic paint.

2 A playpen is not essential but some parents find it useful. It can be moved around the house as required and keeps a baby safe whilst allowing it some freedom.

3 A safety gate is essential where there are stairs or steep steps. An adjustable gate can block different widths of openings and staircases, so this type is more versatile than a fixed barrier. The bars should always be upright to discourage a toddler from climbing, and they should be between 75 mm and 100 mm apart. Window guards should have vertical bars that can be removed in the event of fire.

4 All fires should be guarded where there are children under the age of 12. A sturdy fireguard that can be fixed to the wall, floor or fireplace is preferable to a free-standing guard that can be knocked over. Some fireguards will extend to fit different widths of fireplace. Choose a guard that has a fine mesh. A top protective ledge is advisable. This prevents toys from being thrown over and on to the fire.

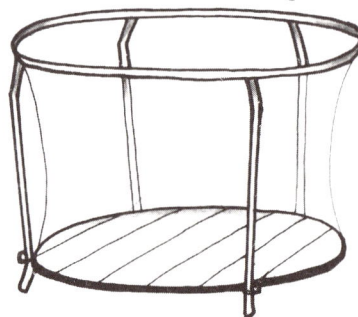

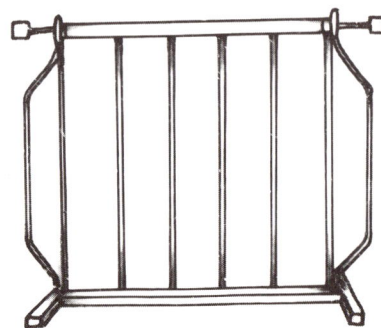

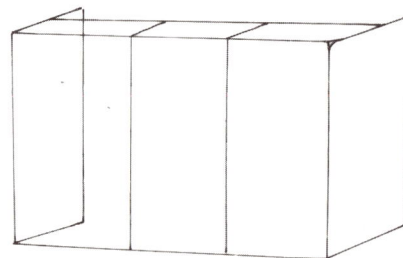

Choosing baby clothes

There is a wide range of colourful and exciting baby clothes available in a variety of different fabrics, and today's parents can have great fun in buying and making their baby's layette. A layette is the complete outfit of clothes required for a new-born baby. It is a mistake to collect too many "first size" clothes. A baby grows quickly and will soon outgrow the first size of clothing. Friends and relations will often buy clothes as a present for the new baby, and it is wise to see what unexpected gifts arrive before accumulating too large a layette.

Here are some points to consider when choosing baby clothes.

1 Baby clothes should be soft so that they will not chafe or rub.

2 They should be warm, comfortable to wear and light in weight. Always look for machine-washable items that do not need ironing.

3 Babystretch garments, which have feet and mittens included, are ideal. There are no gaps at the waist and they are "roomy" enough to allow plenty of movement. They can be worn by day and night therefore they are also very economical.

4 Baby clothes should be easy to put on and take off. Wrap-around clothes, or garments with a loose envelope neck, are suitable. Some baby clothes pull up over the legs and have "popper" or Velcro fastenings.

5 Suitable fabrics for baby clothes are:
stretch terry towelling;
washable knitted fabrics;
cotton jersey;
Viyella;
Clydella;
Winceyette;
cotton/nylon mixtures;
acrylic;
nylon. (This is a non-absorbent fabric and therefore is unsuitable for nightwear.)

6 Hand-knitted garments should have loose neck and wrist edges, no bulky seams, ridges or bobbles and smooth

buttons which are very firmly attached. A baby may trap his fingers or toes in holes so open, lacy patterns should be avoided. Loose ribbons or wool strings should also be avoided

Here is a suggested minimum layette for a first baby.

2 shawls or baby blankets;
5 all-in-one stretch towelling suits with feet and mittens *or*
3 stretch towelling suits and 2 full length nightgowns;
3 matinee jackets;
3 vests;
2 hats.

A winter baby may also need:
2 sleeping bags with hoods;
2 pram suits (jacket, leggings, hood and mittens).

A word about nappies

There are many different types of nappies available. Some are more expensive than others. Parents will select the kind that suits their pocket and way of life best. A combination of disposable nappies during the day and terry towelling nappies during the night is often chosen.

Here are some points to consider when choosing nappies.
1 Terry or Turkish towelling nappies are expensive to buy but they are soft, absorbent and hard wearing. They can be bought as hemmed 60 cm squares, or as triangular-shaped fitted nappies. Square nappies are fastened with special locking safety pins. Fitted nappies are less bulky than square ones, look neater when worn and allow greater freedom of movement, but they are more expensive to buy. They are fastened with "popper" type studs or locking safety pins. Good quality towelling nappies feel heavy and thick.
2 Muslin nappies are very soft and fine. They can be used by themselves or as an inside lining to terry towelling nappies. They are not very absorbent but are suitable for a baby with a sensitive skin.
3 Disposable bonded fabric nappy liners can be used inside towelling nappies. They are convenient and easy to

use, and will catch most of the baby's motion. With each nappy change, the disposable liner can be removed and flushed down the lavatory.

4 One-way nappy liners can be used inside towelling nappies. They are placed next to the baby's skin. The urine filters through the one-way liner and into the absorbent nappy, so keeping the baby dry and comfortable. One-way liners help to prevent nappy rash. They can be used at night only or during the day as well. These nappy liners are washable and can be used over and over again.

5 Disposable nappies can be bought in packs or as a long roll that can be cut into suitable lengths. They are expensive to buy but are a labour-saving luxury which many parents consider invaluable. They can be used with specially fitted waterproof pants. Most disposable nappies can be flushed down the lavatory, but **do check** first.

When a particular type of nappy protection has been selected, an adequate supply must be included in the layette.

A new-born baby will need either:

| 24 terry towelling squares or fitted nappies | 4 pairs of waterproof pants 6 special nappy pins | ➡ OR ➡ | a good supply of disposable nappies (allow 6 per day) | 4 pairs of waterproof pants |

If terry towelling nappies are chosen, the following may also be required:

| 6 muslin nappies ➡ | 4 one-way nappy liners | DISPOSABLE fabric-bonded NAPPY LINERS ❀ |

Preparing for the baby's arrival

A father will want to be especially helpful and considerate during his wife's pregnancy. He may choose to share the housework and do some of the heavy shopping, so that the mother-to-be does not overtire herself. Lifting heavy objects, moving furniture, carrying and hanging out the washing are all practical ways in which a considerate husband can help during pregnancy.

The mother and father will spend much time thinking and talking about their baby and planning for its arrival.

Here are some of the preparations they will want to make together. Try to add to the list.

1 Planning and decorating the nursery.

2 Choosing furniture, clothes and equipment for the baby.

3 Preparing a short list of favourite names.

4 Attending relaxation and child care classes.

5 Starting a scrapbook of things to remember, e.g. the date of "quickening", photographs of pregnant mother and expectant father.

6 Making arrangements for the birth, e.g. checking that everything is ready for a home confinement or having a bag packed for a quick departure to hospital.

7 Planning the help that will be needed in the home after the birth of the baby.

8 Being prepared for emergencies. All necessary telephone numbers should be at hand, together with money if a public telephone has to be used.

Think and Do

1. List **four** fabrics which are suitable for baby clothes. What points should be remembered when hand-knitting baby garments?

2. What precautions can be taken to avoid accidents to a baby, in:

a. the home;

b. the garden;

c. the bath;

d. the pram or pushchair?

3. List the advantages and disadvantages of using:

a. disposable nappies;

b. terry towelling nappies.

4. Give advice on choosing bedding for a baby. What amounts would be required for a first baby, and how can sensible economies be made?

5. List *ten* items you would expect to find in a baby basket.

6. Ask your mother and grandmother to describe the type of baby clothing they used to have for their children. Try to find photographs of yourself as a baby, and family christening snapshots. How have baby clothes changed during the last 50 years?

7. Write a paragraph on each of the following:

a. maternity benefits;

b. suitable floor coverings for a nursery;

c. collecting a layette;

d. choosing a pram.

8. List the preparations that a young couple would make when expecting the birth of their first baby.

9. Find out the current price of:

a. a pair of plastic baby pants;

b. a 200 g container of zinc and castor oil cream;

c. a cellular cotton baby blanket;

d. a baby harness with separate walking rein;

e. a "baby buggy" type pushchair;

f. a fireguard;

g. a stretch towelling all-in-one baby suit;

h. a pack of one-way nappy liners;

i. a box of baby swabs;

j. a "lobster pot" playpen.

10. Look through magazines and catalogues and find a picture of a well-designed cot. Stick it neatly into your notebook and underneath list the points you would look for when choosing a cot.

Childbirth

A human baby spends nine months growing and developing in its mother's uterus. The actual length of pregnancy or **gestation** is 266 days from the day of conception. Since it is not always possible to know exactly when conception occurred, the likely date of a birth is calculated as being 40 weeks from the first day of the last menstrual period.

By the end of pregnancy the baby is usually lying low in the uterus with its head downwards and its body in a crouched or curled position. The chin rests on the chest. If the baby has not settled into this position, a doctor can help by gently turning and manoeuvring it into place. Sometimes a baby lies with its bottom downwards. This is called the "breech" position. If a doctor is not able to turn the baby, it can be born in this position, and is known as a **breech birth**.

Home and hospital confinements

Early in her pregnancy a mother must decide where she would like her baby to be born. She may choose to:

stay at home

go to a private nursing home or maternity home

go to hospital

Some maternity hospitals have special general practitioner units where a mother can be attended by her own doctor or midwife.

A doctor will advise against a home confinement if:

a the mother is aged 35 years or over;

b it is a first baby;

c there is a history of complications in pregnancy or difficulties in labour;

d twins or multiple births are expected;

    e the mother has a medical condition that requires monitoring e.g. diabetes, toxaemia, tuberculosis, kidney disease, a heart disorder;

    f the baby may be at risk because of the Rhesus factor;

    g there has been a previous abortion, miscarriage, stillbirth or Caesarean section;

    h the home condition is unsuitable for the delivery of the baby or the post-natal care of the mother.

A home confinement can be considered by a healthy young woman having her second or third baby, who did not have problems or complications with her previous pregnancies and confinements.

    Here are some of the advantages of having a baby at home.

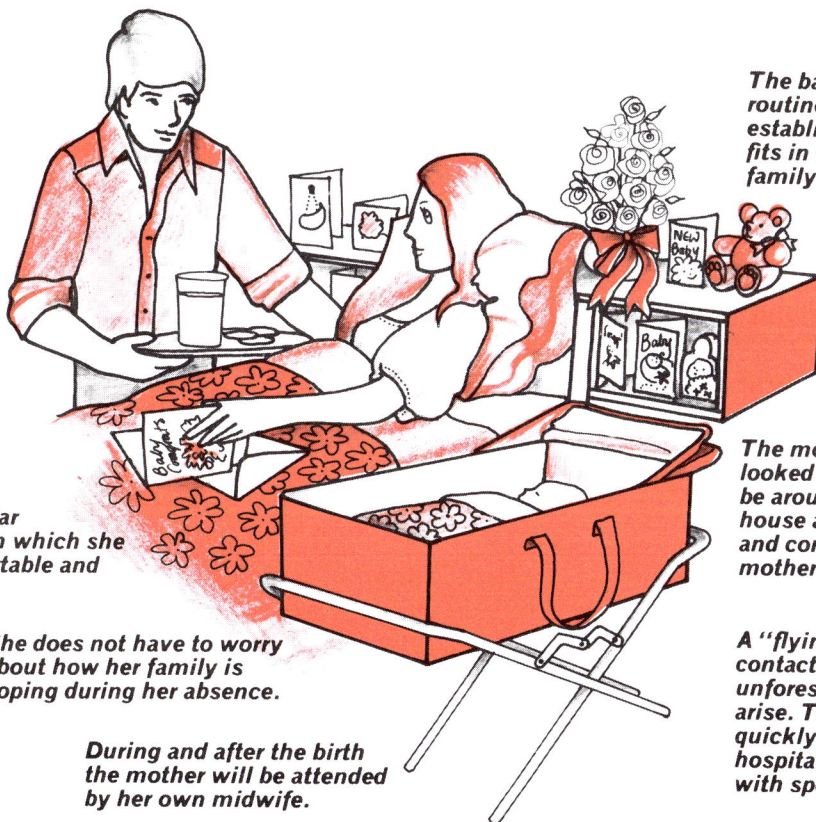

The baby is always near. A routine can be quickly established so that the baby fits in with the rest of the family.

A mother is with her husband and family, making the birth a shared event.

The mother will be well looked after. Someone will be around to help in the house and to ensure rest and constant care for the mother and baby.

A "flying squad" can be contacted should unforeseen complications arise. The mother can be quickly transferred to a hospital or treated at home with specialized equipment.

She is in familiar surroundings in which she can feel comfortable and relaxed.

She does not have to worry about how her family is coping during her absence.

During and after the birth the mother will be attended by her own midwife.

Here are some of the advantages of having a baby in a hospital.

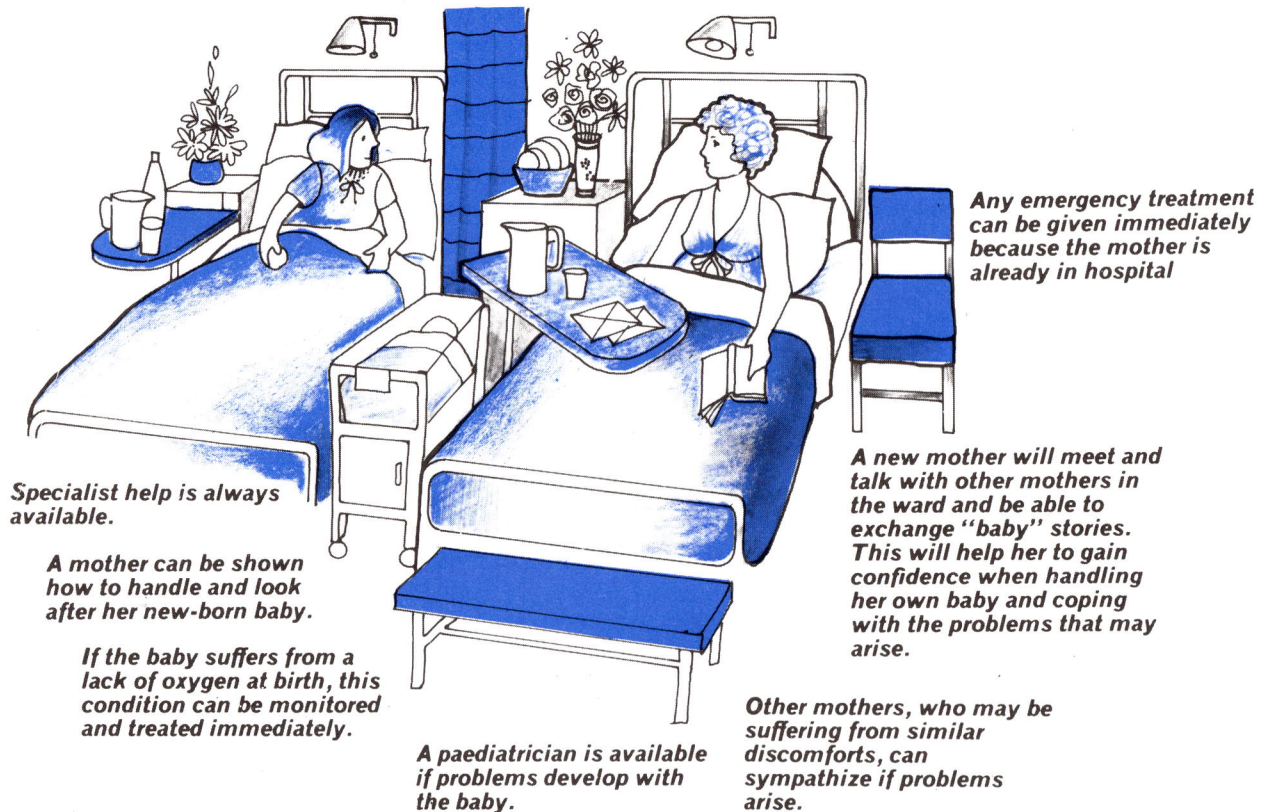

Specialist help is always available.

A mother can be shown how to handle and look after her new-born baby.

If the baby suffers from a lack of oxygen at birth, this condition can be monitored and treated immediately.

A paediatrician is available if problems develop with the baby.

Any emergency treatment can be given immediately because the mother is already in hospital

A new mother will meet and talk with other mothers in the ward and be able to exchange "baby" stories. This will help her to gain confidence when handling her own baby and coping with the problems that may arise.

Other mothers, who may be suffering from similar discomforts, can sympathize if problems arise.

It is quite normal for a mother who has been advised to have her baby in hospital for medical reasons, to have the delivery in hospital and then be transferred home, usually after 48 hours. This is dependent on the health of the mother and baby and whether the home conditions are suitable for post-natal care. The hospital will need to check that a midwife can visit the mother and baby regularly, and that there is someone available to look after the housekeeping requirements leaving the mother free to rest. This is an ideal arrangement for many mothers because it combines the best of both worlds. The mother and baby have the benefit of skilled staff with specialized equipment for the actual delivery, but can then enjoy and share the "getting to know each other" period with their family, in the comfort of their own home.

If problems do arise during the delivery in hospital, a mother can relax in the knowledge that expert help is at hand, and she and her baby will be able to remain in hospital until the doctors are satisfied that all is well.

Relieving pain during childbirth

When a mother is actually giving birth to her baby, she is in *labour*. Labour, as the name suggests, is hard work. It is the process during which the muscles of the uterus and abdomen push the baby out through the cervix and vagina. The length of labour can vary considerably. It is always longer for a first baby. Second and subsequent deliveries are shorter and easier.

The rhythmic movements of the muscles during childbirth are called *contractions*. Labour contractions start as vague feelings of discomfort which come and go. As the length and strength of each contraction increases, the mother may need help to cope with the pain she is experiencing. During relaxation classes a mother is told exactly what will happen during labour. This knowledge is intended to give her confidence, and an understanding that will help her accept the painful build up of contractions. Classes in natural childbirth aim at relieving pain during labour by helping a mother to control her contractions. Various pain-relieving techniques are taught, such as:

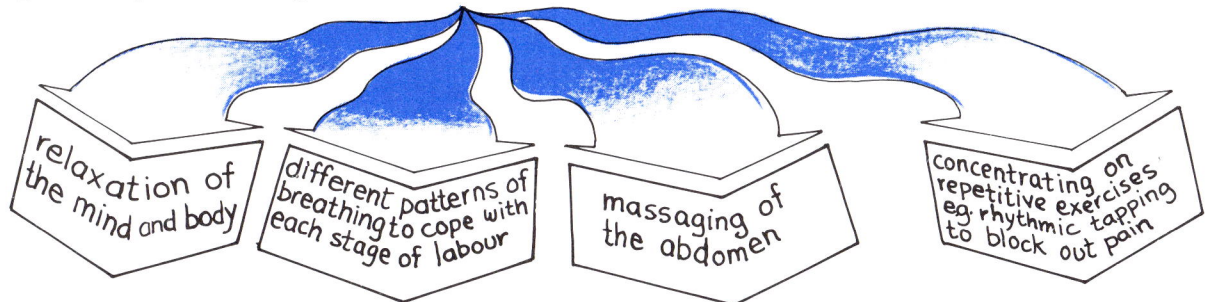

relaxation of the mind and body

different patterns of breathing to cope with each stage of labour

massaging of the abdomen

concentrating on repetitive exercises eg. rhythmic tapping to block out pain

If, however, a mother is becoming tense and distressed during labour, she can be helped with drugs.

Type of drug	Effect
A sedative	This helps the mother to relax by calming the nerves and relieving tension.
A hypnotic drug	This sends the mother to sleep.
An analgesic	This is normally given by injection. It helps the mother to relax and relieves pain.
An anaesthetic	This is inhaled through a mask. It dulls pain.
An epidural anaesthetic	This is a painkiller which is injected into the space around the spinal cord. It numbs the pain of contractions by anaesthetizing the nerves that carry sensations of pain to the brain. This type of anaesthetic does not harm the baby, and leaves the mother fully conscious.

The start of labour

Before labour actually starts a mother may be aware of a heavy ache in her abdomen, thighs or back, or she may suffer from niggling little discomforts that she has not felt before. Sometimes a sudden burst of activity introduces the onset of labour, and a mother may feel unusually fit and energetic. These are outward signs that hormones are being secreted to trigger off the labour mechanism.

There are 3 signs that labour has started:

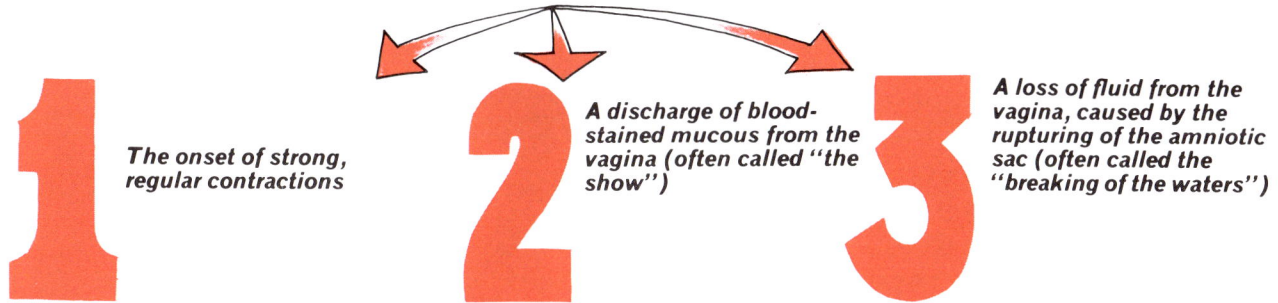

1 *The onset of strong, regular contractions*

2 *A discharge of blood-stained mucous from the vagina (often called "the show")*

3 *A loss of fluid from the vagina, caused by the rupturing of the amniotic sac (often called the "breaking of the waters")*

A mother should go into hospital or send for the midwife when her contractions get longer, stronger and more frequent.

The stages of labour

Labour can be divided into 3 stages.

1 Dilation ⇒⇒ **2** Expulsion ⇒⇒ **3** Placental

The **dilation** or first stage of labour is a long, slow process. The cervix or neck of the uterus gradually opens, and strong muscular contractions pull it upwards and outwards over the head of the baby. These contractions start slowly but build up in intensity, becoming more frequent. When the cervix is fully dilated, the mother experiences a strong urge to bear down or start to push the baby out.

It is during the second stage of labour that the hard work begins. With each contraction the mother bears down, and the baby is slowly pushed through the fully dilated cervix and down the vagina. As the baby's head emerges through the vaginal opening the mother is instructed to stop pushing, so that the baby's shoulders can be manoeuvred into the best position for the birth. The rest of the body follows easily. The new-born baby is placed on the mother's abdomen, whilst still attached to the mother by the umbilical cord. This act seems to ease the **expulsion** of the placenta during the final stage of labour.

The newly born baby is smeared with blood and covered in a greasy substance called **vernix**. When the baby starts to breathe, the pulse in the umbilical cord weakens and then stops altogether. The cord is clamped or tied tightly in two places and cut between the clamps. The baby, who is blue at birth, gradually turns a healthy pink colour.

The mother is usually given an injection after the baby's head has been born. This helps the uterus to contract, so that the placenta or after-birth, the spongy substance which has helped to nourish the unborn baby in the uterus, can be expelled easily. This is the **placental** or third stage of labour and marks the end of the birth.

Other types of birth

A **forceps delivery** may be used if there is a delay in the second stage of labour. Sometimes a mother is not able to bear down efficiently and needs help to push out the baby. Occasionally the baby's head gets stuck or there may be difficulty with a breech birth. Any undue delay could harm the baby who may suffer from a lack of oxygen. Forceps resemble large metal spoons. They are designed to fit around the baby's head without causing any damage to the mother or baby. The baby can then be gently pulled out. Forceps are only used if the baby is well down in the pelvis and can be helped out easily.

If the baby is stuck high in the mother's pelvis and labour is not progressing smoothly, a **Caesarean delivery** may be used. This involves surgery and is usually done under a general anaesthetic. A small cut is made across the lower part of the mother's abdomen, and the baby is delivered through the wall of the uterus. A Caesarean delivery is also used when normal delivery by the natural passages would be difficult or unwise.

Sometimes there may be medical reasons that make it necessary to induce labour or trigger it off artificially. **Induction of labour** can be done by breaking the membranes of the amniotic sac, and by giving the mother a hormone which causes the uterus to contract.

How the father can help during childbirth

Although it is the mother who is actively involved in the pregnancy, labour and delivery of a baby, there are many ways in which the father can help. The birth of a baby should be a shared event. Research has shown that where the father participates throughout pregnancy and the birth, he becomes more involved with the baby and a deeper father-child relationship often develops.

The presence of the father can affect the actual progress of a birth. The mother will feel more relaxed and confident, and may therefore require fewer pain-relieving drugs. If she begins to feel distressed by the contractions, the father can offer reassurance and encouragement. If the couple have attended ante-natal classes together, the father can give positive help during labour by reminding the mother about breathing patterns and the importance of relaxation. If the mother is having her baby at home he can see that she is as comfortable as possible by massaging her abdomen and back, fetching extra blankets if she feels cold, or getting her a drink if she feels thirsty.

Think and Do

1. In your notebook, list the advantages of having a baby in hospital.
2. How can a father help during the birth of his baby?
3. Copy the following diagram into your notebook and write a suitable sentence in each of the boxes.

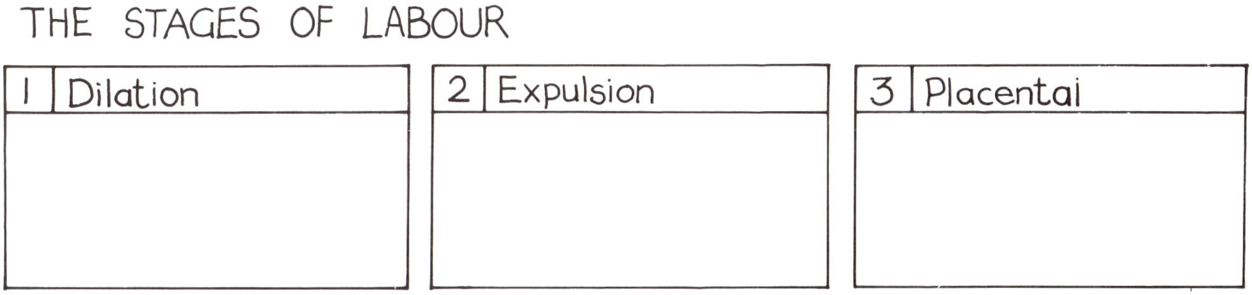

THE STAGES OF LABOUR

1 Dilation	2 Expulsion	3 Placentai

4. Explain what is meant by each of the following:

a. "the breaking of the waters";

b. an induced birth;

c. an epidural anaesthetic.

5. Copy the following sentences into your notebook. Say whether each one is *true* or *false*.

a. The rhythmic movements of the muscles during child-birth are called contractions.

b. An anaesthetic drug is given by injection.

c. A blood-stained discharge from the vagina is an indication that labour has started.

d. The second stage of labour is called the dilation stage.

e. A "breech" position is when the baby is lying head downwards in the uterus.

6. How can a mother tell that labour is starting? When is it advisable for her to go into hospital or send for the midwife?

7. Visit your school and local libraries and find out all you can about childbirth through the ages.

8. How can pain be relieved during childbirth?

9. Copy out this crossword and complete it.

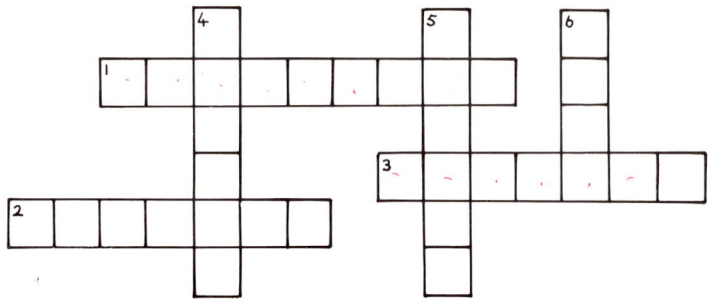

Clues across

1. The type of delivery used when a baby is born through the abdominal and uterine walls.

2. This person attends mothers during childbirth.

3. May be used to help deliver a baby.

Clues down

4. New-born babies are covered with this.

5. Another name for childbirth.

6. The colour of a new-born baby.

10. Say what happens to each of the following during labour:

a. the amniotic sac;

b. the cervix;

c. the umbilical cord;

d. the placenta.

Care of the new-born baby

Some hospitals still whisk a new-born baby away from its mother, and limit contact between mother and baby to rigid feeding and changing time-tables. The father may only be able to see his child at visiting times, and then may be warned "not to touch". Happily, such hospitals seem to be in the minority. Modern maternity units keep mother and baby together, and they are able to get to know each other in a relaxed and happy atmosphere.

Most doctors and midwives now recognize the importance of a mother and father touching and fondling their new-born baby immediately after the birth. This creates a maternal and paternal bond, which may be helpful in preventing "baby battering" during periods of stress. Some maternity units take photographs of each newly born baby and give one copy to the mother and one to the father. These become precious reminders of their baby's birth. Fondling and touching a baby presents no problems during a home confinement. The baby is always at hand, and both mother and father can handle and caress it whenever they wish.

If a mother intends to breast-feed her baby, she is likely to be more successful if she puts the baby to the breast within four hours of the birth. A new-born baby has a natural sucking action, which seems to diminish with time. If there is a delay in starting to breast-feed, problems are more likely to occur.

All these points highlight the importance of a baby's first few hours.

Registering a birth

There are certain legal procedures which have to be attended to after the birth of a baby.

The Registrar of Births and Deaths (the Registrar of Births, Deaths and Marriages in Scotland) is notified when a baby is born. This is usually done by the doctor or midwife. In addition, a birth, whether live or stillborn, should be registered at the Registry Office in the district where the baby is born. This should be done in the six weeks immediately after the birth. A birth certificate will be issued in the baby's name.

Claiming benefits

A child benefit can be claimed immediately after a birth, by application to the local Social Security Office. Paid weekly at the nearest Post Office, it is available for each child.

A mother is entitled to claim free prescriptions and dental treatment for herself, for one year after the birth of a baby. Free milk and vitamins are provided for children under school age in low income families. They are also given to families with three or more children under school age, whatever the income.

Feeding a baby

A new-born baby will divide most of his day between eating and sleeping. He will require food approximately every four hours, though this can vary with the size of the baby. A tiny baby will need food more frequently than a large baby. At first, it is a good idea for parents to try a regular four-hourly routine of feeding, e.g. 6 a.m.; 10 a.m.; 2 p.m.; 6 p.m.; 10 p.m.; 2 a.m. and then to adapt this pattern to suit their baby's needs. It is not necessary to waken a sleeping baby because it happens to be time for the next feeding session, and in a similar way, it is cruel to refuse to feed a hungry baby just because he has woken up too early. A mother and father should let a new-born baby choose the feeding schedule that he prefers. Some babies will quickly drop the 2 a.m. feed and sleep right through the night until the early hours of the morning. Other babies require regular feeding through the night until they are several weeks old. If meals are unhurried, relaxed, happy occasions, a baby will quickly settle into his own feeding pattern.

A new-born baby requires milk. It is the food on which babies thrive. This can be human breast milk or a form of cow's milk which is specially prepared for babies. Milk is easily digested and is a highly nutritious food containing:

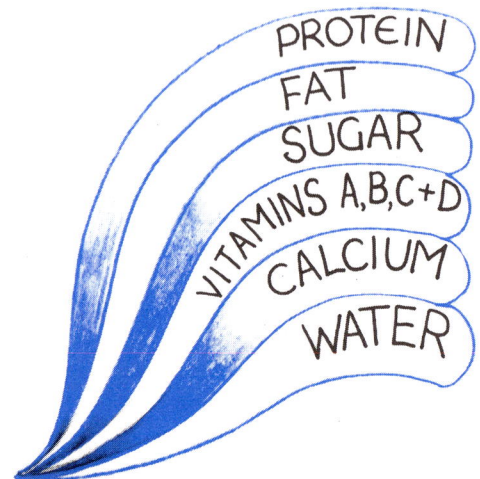

PROTEIN
FAT
SUGAR
VITAMINS A, B, C + D
CALCIUM
WATER

Breast-feeding

Breast-feeding is nature's way of providing food for the very young, but not every mother wants to breast-feed her baby, and sometimes a mother wishes to but is unable.

Here are some of the advantages and disadvantages of breast-feeding.

Advantages	*Disadvantages*

Advantages

1 Breast milk is highly nutritious. It is the right strength, and particularly suitable for new-born babies.
2 It is pure and free from any infection.
3 A breast-fed baby receives an immunity from disease for the first few months of his life. This benefit is believed to be due to the **colostrum** (the yellow fluid present immediately after the birth) in the breasts.
4 Breast milk is warm and the correct temperature for a young baby.
5 Breast-feeding is a convenient method. Time can be saved by not having to sterilize bottles and prepare feeds.
6 Breast milk is free. There is no need to buy feeding and sterilizing equipment.
7 Breast-feeding can be emotionally satisfying. A special bond is forged between mother and baby.
8 A suckling baby causes the uterine walls to contract. Breast-feeding therefore helps a mother to regain her figure.
9 If a mother is to produce milk and breast-feed successfully, she must eat a nutritious and well-balanced diet, and get plenty of rest and relaxation. This is beneficial for a mother's general health and well-being.
10 A breast-fed baby has less wind than a bottle-fed baby, and seldom becomes overweight.

Disadvantages

1 A mother may dislike the idea of breast-feeding.
2 There may be embarrassment if she is required to breast-feed in public. This can cause problems when travelling.
3 The father is not able to help with feeding the baby, and may feel excluded at meal times. He is not able to relieve a tired mother by taking over one of the night feeds.
4 A mother may wish to return to work quickly, and leave her baby in a crêche or nursery or with a baby-minder or relation.
5 A couple may not want a baby to interfere with their social life, and prefer to leave bottle feeds so that a baby-sitter can feed the baby.
6 Breast-feeding can sometimes:
   a cause the breasts to feel sore, tender or painful;
   b make the nipples crack.
7 A mother may not wish to feel tied down by always having to be present at meal times.

Bottle-feeding

Bottle-feeding is a perfectly satisfactory method of feeding a baby, and if adequate care is taken when sterilizing the equipment and preparing the feeds, a bottle-fed baby will thrive just as well as a breast-fed baby.

A baby may be bottle-fed with:

a any one of a selection of brands of dried milk;

b evaporated or unsweetened tinned milk;

c liquid cow's milk. (This is only suitable for older babies.)

A Child Health Clinic will give advice on which type to choose. Modern brands of dried milk are made to resemble breast milk as much as possible. Some brands contain more salt than others. A dried milk with a *low* salt content is best.

Here are some of the advantages and disadvantages of bottle-feeding.

Advantages	*Disadvantages*
1 Bottle feeds can be prepared in advance and stored in a refrigerator.	*1* Milk is easily contaminated. Unless strict hygiene is observed at all times, a bottle-fed baby may be infected.
2 A mother need not be present at each feed. Father can help out when he is at home, and take advantage of the opportunity to cuddle and play with his baby, or bottles may be left with a relative or friend who is baby-sitting.	*2* The milk, feeding and sterilizing equipment have to be bought.
3 A mother may return to work as soon as she wishes.	*3* The milk for bottle-feeding has to be heated to the correct temperature.
	4 A bottle-fed baby has more wind than a breast-fed baby.

It is essential to keep all bottle-feeding equipment sterile and free from germs. This can be done by:

a immersing the equipment in cold water which is then heated and kept at boiling point for three minutes. If sterilizing with boiling water, you will need a saucepan with a lid. This must be large enough to hold at least two feeding bottles, and deep enough to completely submerge the bottles in the boiling water.

b immersing the equipment in a hypochlorite solution for at least thirty minutes. (A hypochlorite solution

is formed by adding special tablets or Milton liquid to tap water.) If sterilizing with a hypochlorite solution, you will need a plastic, glass or china container with a lid. This must be large enough to hold at least two feeding bottles, and deep enough to completely submerge the bottles in the sterilizing solution. Some sterilizing units are sold complete with feeding bottles and other necessary accessories, and are large enough to hold four bottles.

Other equipment that will be needed when bottle-feeding.

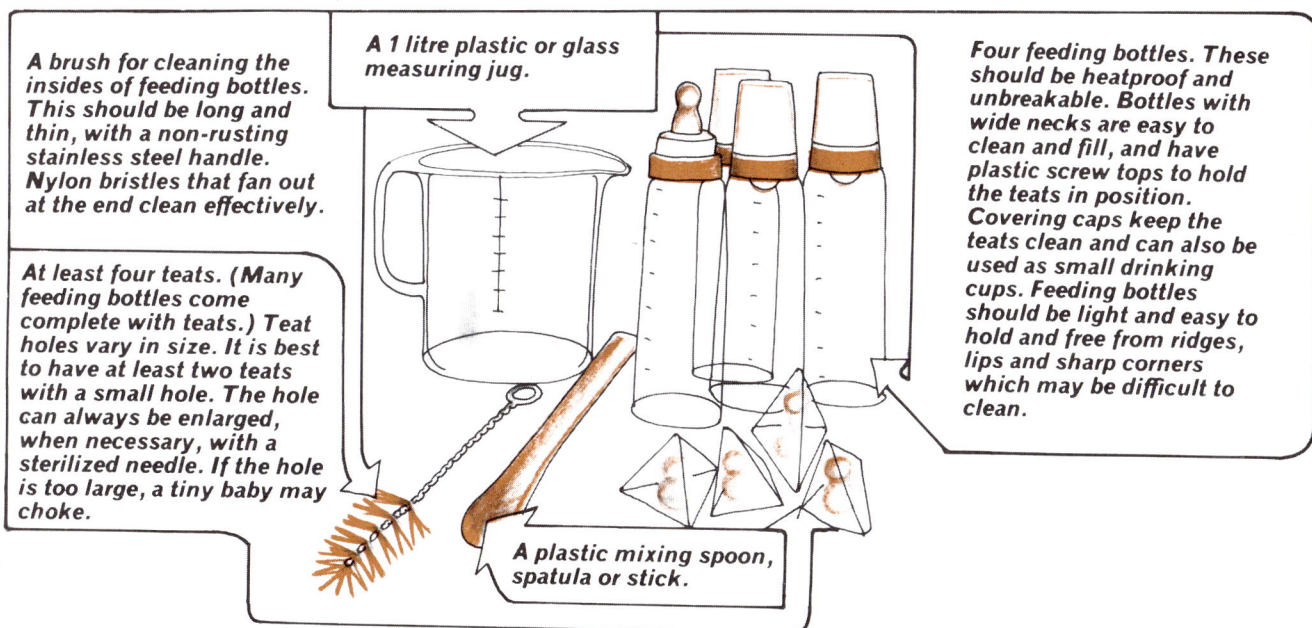

A brush for cleaning the insides of feeding bottles. This should be long and thin, with a non-rusting stainless steel handle. Nylon bristles that fan out at the end clean effectively.

A 1 litre plastic or glass measuring jug.

Four feeding bottles. These should be heatproof and unbreakable. Bottles with wide necks are easy to clean and fill, and have plastic screw tops to hold the teats in position. Covering caps keep the teats clean and can also be used as small drinking cups. Feeding bottles should be light and easy to hold and free from ridges, lips and sharp corners which may be difficult to clean.

At least four teats. (Many feeding bottles come complete with teats.) Teat holes vary in size. It is best to have at least two teats with a small hole. The hole can always be enlarged, when necessary, with a sterilized needle. If the hole is too large, a tiny baby may choke.

A plastic mixing spoon, spatula or stick.

How to take care of bottle-feeding equipment

1 After each feed:
   a rinse all equipment in cold water;
   b wash thoroughly in hot water;
   c rinse again in clear water.

2 Scrub feeding bottles *inside* and *outside* with a bottle brush. Check that the rims of bottles are clean.

3 Rinse teats and then rub them with salt. Salt removes traces of butter fat and helps to clear the holes. Re-rinse.

4 After thoroughly cleaning *all* pieces of equipment:
- **a** store them in a clean container until they can be sterilized in boiling water *or*
- **b** place them in the hypochlorite solution until needed for the next feed.

How to prepare a bottle feed

1 Wash hands thoroughly in hot, soapy water, and then dry on a clean towel.

2 Check that all the necessary equipment is sterile.

3 Before preparing a feed for a new-born baby, read the instructions on the packet or tin of milk, so that you are certain what strength of milk you should be preparing. Do not alter the suggested milk/water proportion, unless a doctor has advised you to do so. The wrong concentration of milk can be dangerous for a new-born baby.

4 Measure dried milk with the specially provided spoon or scoop. Do not pack the milk powder into the spoon, and level off each measure carefully with a knife.

Place the milk powder into the sterile measuring jug. Add sugar, if required. Mix to a smooth cream with a small amount of *boiled* water. Continue to add boiled water, stirring all the time, until the correct level on the measure has been reached. If *boiling* water is used, the vitamin C in the milk will be destroyed. Always mix a bottle feed with water which has been boiled and left to cool a little.

5 Pour the milk into a sterilized feeding bottle. Put the teat into position and cover with the cap.

6 Cool the milk by holding the bottle under a running cold tap. A bottle feed should feel warm when sprinkled on the back of the hand.

7 If evaporated milk is being used, put the required amount of milk into a saucepan. Add sugar and water. Boil the mixture for three minutes. Pour the milk into a sterilized feeding bottle. Put the teat into position and cover with the cap. This milk is lacking in vitamin C, and vitamin drops should be given each day to correct the deficiency (see chapter 8).

8 If making more than one feed at once, store the extra bottles in a refrigerator. When each one is needed, stand the

levelling off a spoon

feeding bottle with teat in position

feeding bottle covered by a cap

bottle in a saucepan or jug of hot water, until the milk reaches the required temperature.

An electric bottle warmer is a useful piece of equipment, especially when preparing night feeds. It is thermostatically controlled and will switch off when the bottle reaches the correct temperature.

A word of warning

A baby should **never** be left to feed himself from a propped up bottle. This can be very dangerous.

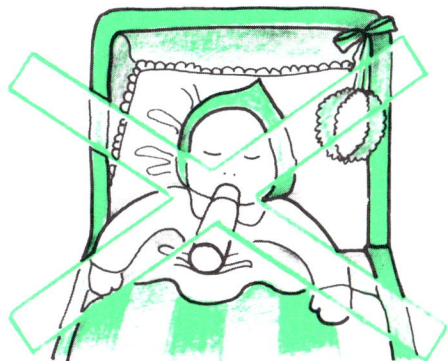

He may develop an infection of the middle ear if milk or vomit enters the canal which joins the back of the throat to the middle ear.

He will not receive the affection and security that a parent can offer whilst nursing and feeding the baby.

He may swallow a lot of air.

He may vomit, splutter and choke.

How to bring up a baby's wind

Halfway through each feed, a baby should have a rest from sucking, so that he can bring up any air bubbles which he has swallowed. To help a baby bring up wind:

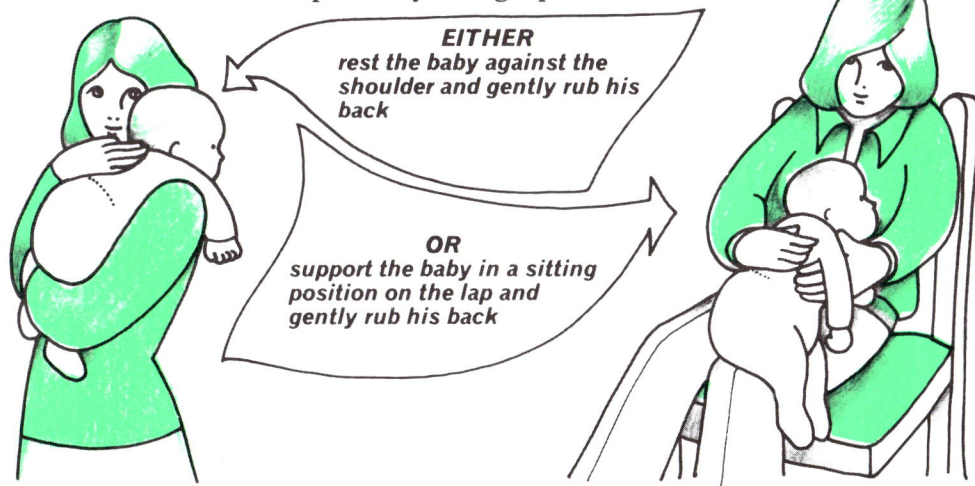

EITHER rest the baby against the shoulder and gently rub his back

OR support the baby in a sitting position on the lap and gently rub his back

This should be repeated at the end of each feed. If a baby is being bottle-fed, slant the bottle downwards so that the teat and neck of the bottle are always full of milk. This stops the baby from sucking too much air into his stomach.

Keeping a baby clean

The skin of a new-born baby is very soft, smooth and delicate, and should be handled carefully. A daily bath is not essential but it does help to keep a baby fresh, clean and comfortable. A baby should be bathed **before** a meal, never after one. Some parents find it convenient to bath their baby before the 10 a.m. feed, and others prefer to save the bath until the early evening, so that the baby will sleep better during the night.

How to bath a baby

1 Prepare the room and equipment first.
  a Make sure the room is warm.
  b Prevent draughts by closing windows and doors.
  c Check that everything you need is placed nearby.
  d Fill the baby bath. This can be done by using warm water, or by putting cold water into the bath first and then adding hot water. The bath water should feel comfortably warm when tested with the elbow.

2 Undress the baby and wrap him in a warm towel. Sit down with the baby on your lap.

3 Start with the baby's face and head.
  a Using a soft facecloth or a piece of cotton wool wash the baby's face with clear water.
  b A dirty nose can be cleaned with a twist of cotton wool or a cotton wool swab.
  c Unless the eyes and ears look dirty, they should be left alone. If necessary, small pieces of dampened cotton wool can be used to gently sponge around them.
  d Wash the head using baby soap or shampoo. If a special liquid soapless bath oil has been added to the bath water, there is no need to use anything else. Rinse the scalp and then pat the baby's face and head dry. (If the scalp has patches of cradle-cap, a yellowish waxy material, gently rub olive oil into it.)

4 Unwrap the towel and soap the baby all over, using a face-cloth or your hand. This is not necessary if a bath oil is being used.

5 Lower the baby into the bath, holding him firmly. Your left arm should be across the back of his neck and holding his left shoulder. Your right arm is then free to gently splash the baby with the bath water, and rinse off all the soap. Let the baby have a good kick in the warm water.

6 Carefully lift out the baby and put him back on your lap. Using a towel, pat him dry. Care should be taken to dry thoroughly in the folds and creases of the body. It is not necessary to use talcum powder but if you would like to use a little, apply the talcum powder with your hand, rather than dusting from the container. This stops the baby from breathing powder into his lungs.

Nappy rash

A baby's nappy should be changed frequently if he is to be kept comfortable and free of nappy rash. Nappy rash is a painful condition, when the skin on a baby's bottom becomes red, sore, cracked and covered in tiny spots or blisters. It is caused by the formation of ammonia in the nappy. This chemical then attacks the skin.

To prevent nappy rash:

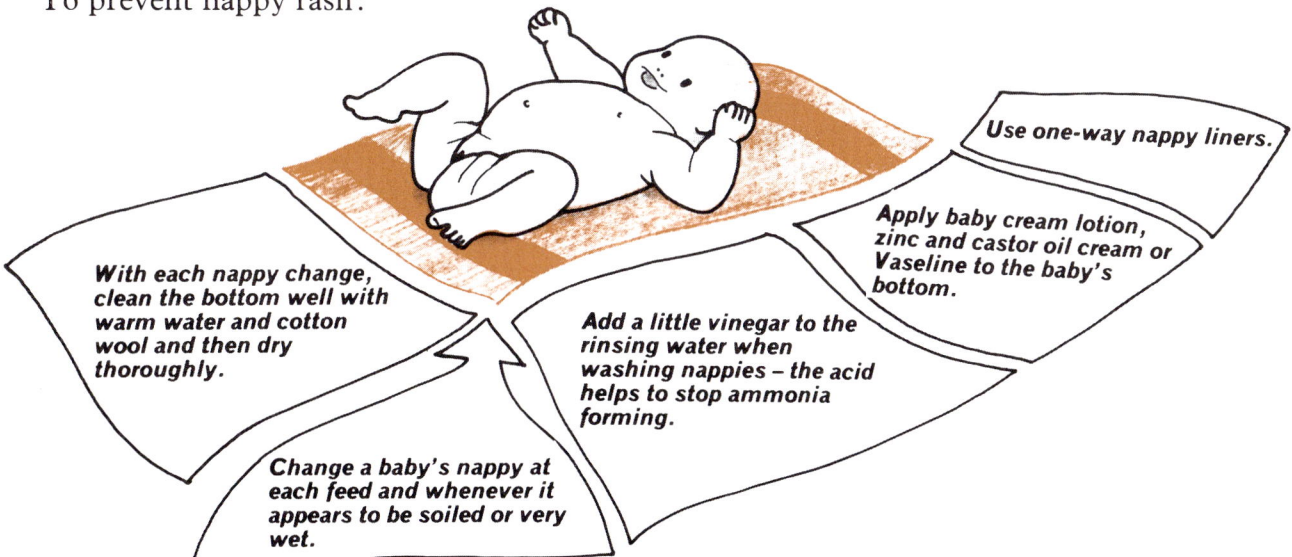

With each nappy change, clean the bottom well with warm water and cotton wool and then dry thoroughly.

Change a baby's nappy at each feed and whenever it appears to be soiled or very wet.

Add a little vinegar to the rinsing water when washing nappies – the acid helps to stop ammonia forming.

Apply baby cream lotion, zinc and castor oil cream or Vaseline to the baby's bottom.

Use one-way nappy liners.

To treat nappy rash:

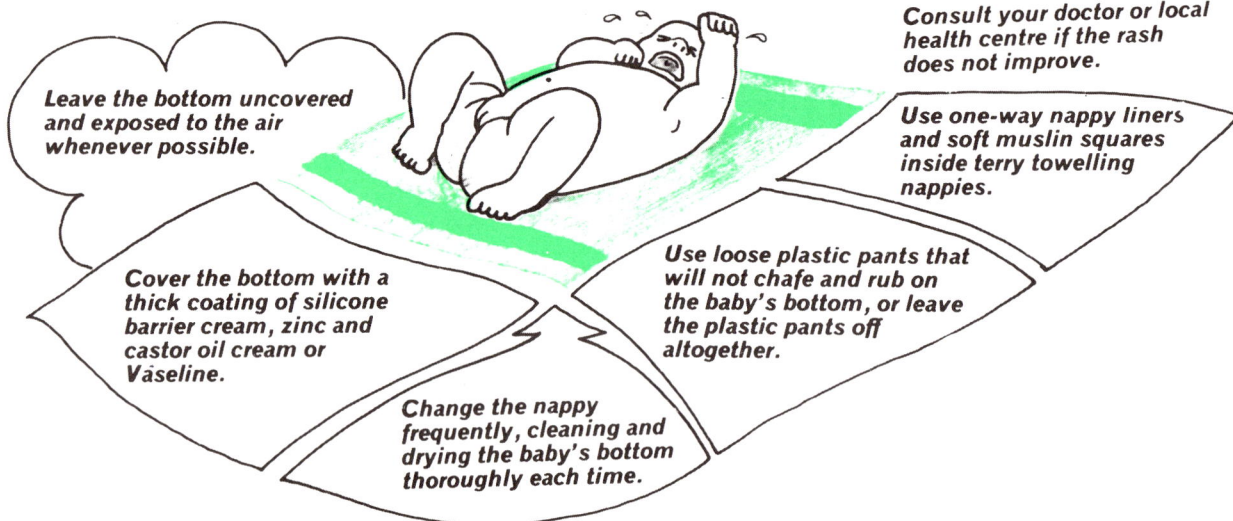

Leave the bottom uncovered and exposed to the air whenever possible.

Consult your doctor or local health centre if the rash does not improve.

Use one-way nappy liners and soft muslin squares inside terry towelling nappies.

Cover the bottom with a thick coating of silicone barrier cream, zinc and castor oil cream or Vaseline.

Use loose plastic pants that will not chafe and rub on the baby's bottom, or leave the plastic pants off altogether.

Change the nappy frequently, cleaning and drying the baby's bottom thoroughly each time.

How to put on a nappy

A disposable nappy is slotted inside the "pockets" of a pair of special waterproof pants. These are then tied or fastened around the baby's waist with "popper" closures.

A terry towelling nappy can be put on in one of three ways.

1 Fold the nappy into a triangle. Place the baby on the folded nappy, with the apex of the triangle between the baby's legs. Bring the three ends of the nappy together, so that the nappy lies flat and taut. Fasten the three layers together using a nappy pin placed horizontally.

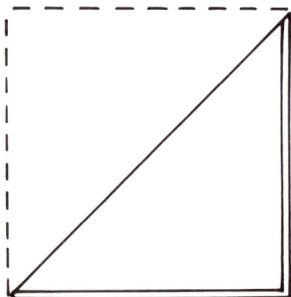

2 Fold the nappy in half to form a rectangle and then fold over one third of it. Place the baby on the thicker part of the nappy. Bring the other half up between the baby's legs and pin it at either side of the waist.

3 Fold the nappy to resemble a kite. Fold the top and bottom points towards the centre. Place the baby so that the narrow point of the nappy comes up between the baby's legs. Bring each side across and fasten the three thicknesses together with one or two nappy pins.

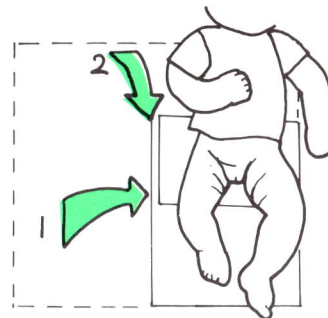

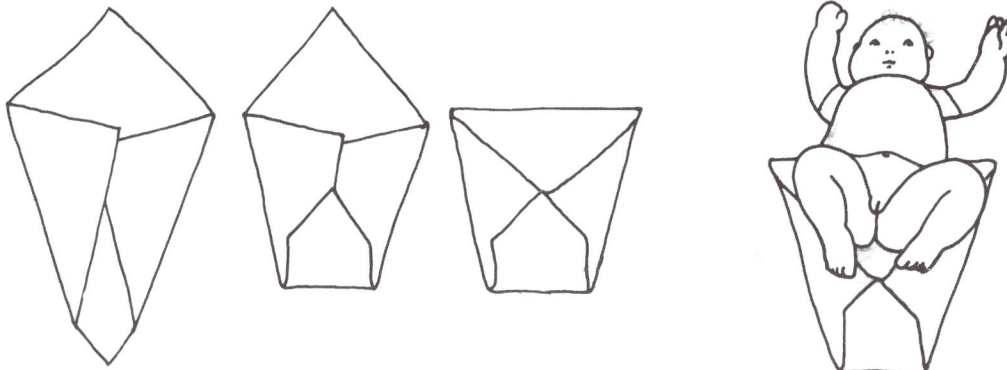

If a one-way nappy liner and a disposable nappy liner are being used with a terry towelling nappy, arrange the layers like this:

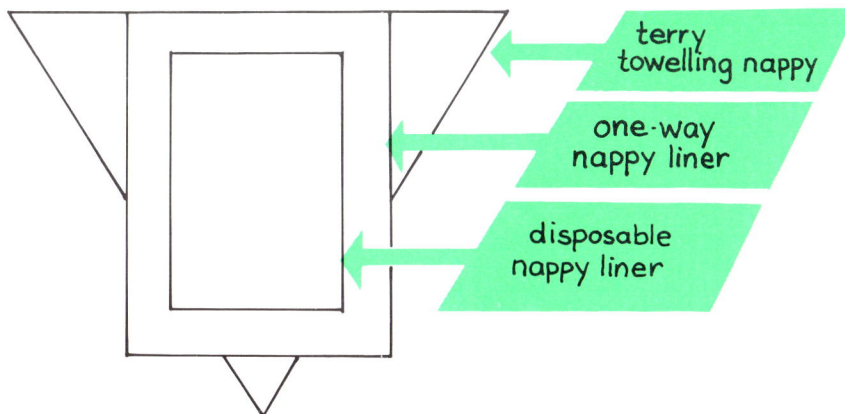

terry towelling nappy

one-way nappy liner

disposable nappy liner

A word about disposable nappies
Some disposable nappies are not completely soluble. If you are in any doubt, do not flush them down the lavatory.

EITHER

OR

burn them in a garden incinerator

enclose them in a strong plastic bag and dispose of them in the dustbin

How to wash a soiled terry towelling nappy
When removing a soiled nappy:

a flush the disposable nappy liner down the lavatory, or shake off as much of the faeces as possible;

b rinse the stained nappy in running cold water;

c cleanse and sterilize the nappy in one of the ways shown in the chart opposite.

It would be uneconomical to wash each nappy as soon as it becomes soiled or wet. Allow them to accumulate until a full washing machine load has been collected. Nappies can be left to soak in cold water and vinegar until they can be dealt with. If washing by hand, complete the wash cycle but do not boil the nappies until several have been collected.

How to dry nappies
Nappies will remain whiter, softer and fresher if they are hung in the fresh air to dry.

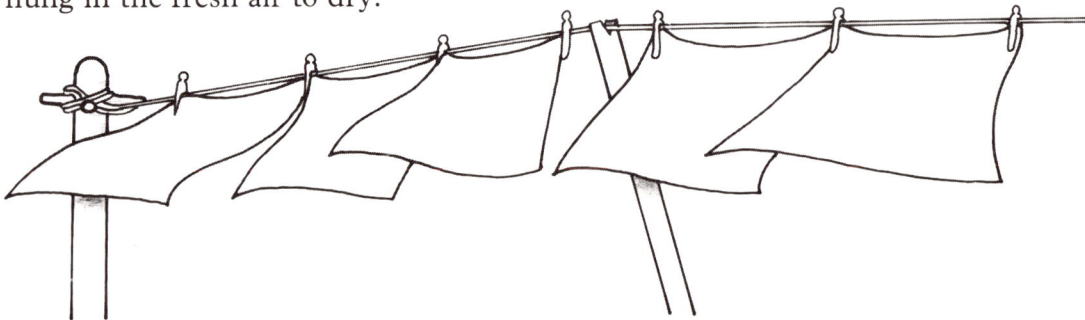

Treatment	Method
Using a chemical solution e.g. Napisan, N.S.P.	Prepare the solution in a plastic bucket. (Always read the directions on the canister carefully.) Soak the nappy in the prepared solution for at least two hours. Rinse thoroughly and dry. This method keeps nappies white, sterile and soft.
Using a washing machine	Leave the nappy to soak in a bucket of cold water plus two tablespoons of vinegar. Wash the nappy in **very hot** water in the washing machine, using soap flakes. Rinse well in hot water. Give a final rinse in cold water with the addition of a fabric softener. Dry.
Washing by hand and boiling	Leave the nappy to soak in a bucket of cold water plus vinegar. Hand wash the nappy in hot water, using soap flakes. Rinse thoroughly in hot water. Boil in clean water for a few minutes. Dry.
Using a laundry or launderette	Many laundries have a nappy service and will collect, launder and return nappies. This is an expensive service. If using a local launderette, always rinse and pre-soak nappies at home first.

If this is not possible, use:

- a tumbler-drier
- a spin-drier
- a drying cabinet
- a "fold away" line drier indoors
- a clothes "horse" frame
- rails that clip over a central heating radiator
- a "fold away" rack drier over the bath

When nappies have to be dried in one of these ways, add a fabric softener to the final rinse. This will help to keep the nappies soft.

Getting to know a new-born baby

A new-born baby will spend most of his time asleep, and will usually only waken when being fed, changed or bathed. Some days he may require less sleep than others, and will lie quietly in his pram or cot, just gazing around, listening to sounds and occasionally waving his arms and moving his legs. During these periods of wakefulness, a baby is learning to use his muscles and is experimenting with and exploring his immediate surroundings.

A young baby should be left to sleep or lie quietly, preferably in the fresh air. His pram should be put in a sheltered place, away from draughts and out of the sunlight. A pram net is useful, especially in the summer months, to protect the baby from flies, bees, wasps and cats.

If the weather is very cold, foggy, damp or wet, a baby should be kept indoors in his pram or cot.

What to do when a baby cries

If a new-born baby cries, it is usually a sign that something is wrong. A parent will quickly learn to distinguish between the different types of distress signals, and will grow accustomed to coping with each one.

Reason for crying	Remedy
The baby is hungry.	If it is over two hours since his last feed, try offering him some more food.
The baby is thirsty.	Give him a drink of plain boiled water.
He has swallowed some wind.	Lift him up and try to relieve the discomfort by one of the methods described earlier.
His nappy is wet or dirty.	Change him.
He is too hot or too cold.	If the baby looks hot, loosen his coverings and fold one sheet back. If the baby feels cold, add another lightweight blanket.
The baby is tired.	Make sure that he is lying comfortably and then leave him.
He feels insecure.	Pick up the baby and cuddle him. Hold him tightly for a few minutes and then put him back in his pram or cot.

If a young baby persists in crying and none of the above remedies help, then try comforting him by:
a rocking him in your arms or in a rocking chair;
b holding him tightly and singing a lullaby;
c laying him across your knees and rubbing his back;
d giving him a sterile dummy to suck.

Fitting a new-born baby into a family unit
A new-born baby can be a demanding individual who often seems to require attention at awkward times of the day. He

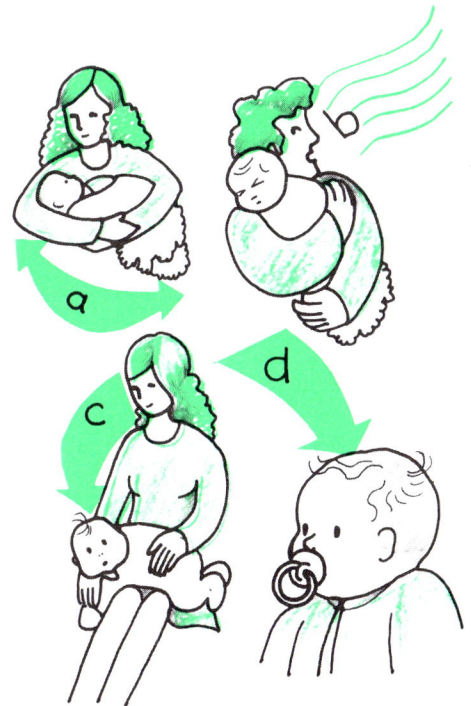

may be fretful at family meal times, and in the evening, when most parents are wanting to relax a little. It is important to see that existing members of the family are not neglected because of the new baby.

Jealousy is easily felt by:

Here are some points to help when fitting a new baby into the family unit.

1 Try to talk to and play with an older child just as much as you did before the baby arrived. Do not let him feel displaced in your affections, or he will resent his baby brother or sister.

2 It is helpful if the new baby can bring a little gift for the older child. This introduces one to the other pleasurably.

3 Let an older child help with the new baby as much as possible so that bathing, changing and feeding activities become happy, relaxed family occasions.

4 Both mother and father should share the responsibilities involved in caring for a family. The unit will become closer and happier if the father:

    a shares the housework, especially at weekends;

    b helps to bath, change and feed the children;

    c shares the night-time duties;

    d finds time to play with, read to, sing to, and watch television with the children;

    e is attentive, understanding and thoughtful to his wife, especially when she is feeling overtired, low and depressed.

5 A new mother should reassure her husband that she:

    a still loves him;

    b needs him;

    c enjoys his company;

    d will not neglect him because of the baby;

    e will not neglect her own health and appearance;

    f enjoys seeing him caring for the baby.

Think and Do

1. List the advantages and disadvantages of breast-feeding.

2. Design a poster that will illustrate the importance of hygiene when caring for a new-born baby.

3. Say how you would:

a. bring up a baby's wind;

b. sterilize a soiled nappy;

c. cool a baby's feeding bottle;

d. test the temperature of a baby's bath water.

4. With the aid of diagrams describe *two* methods of putting on a nappy.

5. Where would you go to:

a. register a birth;

b. claim a child benefit;

c. obtain advice on the brands of dried milk suitable for a baby?

6. What equipment would be needed to bottle-feed a baby? How can this equipment be kept sterile? Why is it dangerous to leave a baby to feed himself from a bottle?

7. Write a paragraph about each of the following:

a. cradle cap;

b. colostrum;

c. hypochlorite solution.

8. What advice would you give to a young parent on:

a. bathing a baby;

b. treating nappy rash;

c. preparing a bottle feed;

d. stopping a baby from crying?

9. How would you prevent other children in a family from feeling jealous of a new baby? Describe ways in which each of the following people can help:

a. mother; *b.* father; *c.* grandparents.

10. Ask your teacher if she can arrange a visit to your local Child Health Clinic. After your visit, write a description of what you saw.

Infancy (birth to 3 years)

Physical growth and development

The first year of a baby's life is marked by a period of rapid bodily growth and development. A baby's physical growth will be affected by:

    a his diet;

    b his weight and length at birth;

    c the height of his parents.

An average child weighs about 3·4 kg at birth and will gain approximately 6 kg in his first year. His weight gain will then slow down.

At two years he will weigh about 12·25 kg:

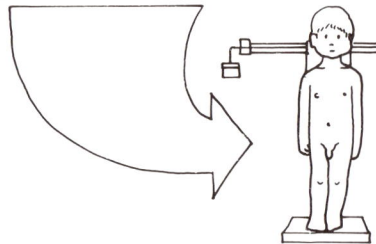

At three years he will weigh about 14·5 kg:

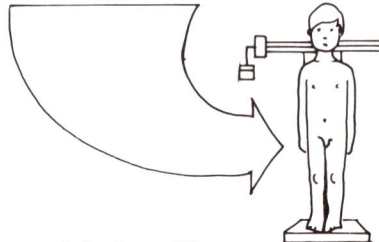

An average child who measures about 54 cm at birth, will grow approximately 20 cm in the first year. His rate of growth will then slow down.

At two years he will measure about 85 cm:

At three years he will measure about 93 cm:

Any child can have a temporary loss in weight, and a child's growth rate and development may suddenly slow down or quicken for no apparent reason, but this need not cause anxiety. Each baby is an individual and will grow and develop at his own rate.

As a baby grows in size, he develops skills. He can be helped to acquire skills by:

having the attention of caring adults who talk and play with him so that he can imitate their behaviour

feeling loved and secure in a happy family relationship

being provided with toys that stimulate his brain and make him aware of his environment

being encouraged and praised when attempting new skills

It is important to remember though, that skills will only be acquired when the brain and nervous system have developed sufficiently. For example, a child will not be able to smile, sit upright unaided, walk, grasp objects, however much he is encouraged and helped, unless his brain has reached the right stage of development so that he is able to acquire each of these skills. A premature baby is one that is born early, and he will therefore be later in developing skills, than a full-term baby, because his brain is not as mature.

A child's ability to master muscular skills will be affected by his particular personality. The determined child, who keeps on experimenting, can be expected to acquire and perfect a new skill earlier than the placid child, who is easily put off by initial failures and difficulties.

A new-born baby:

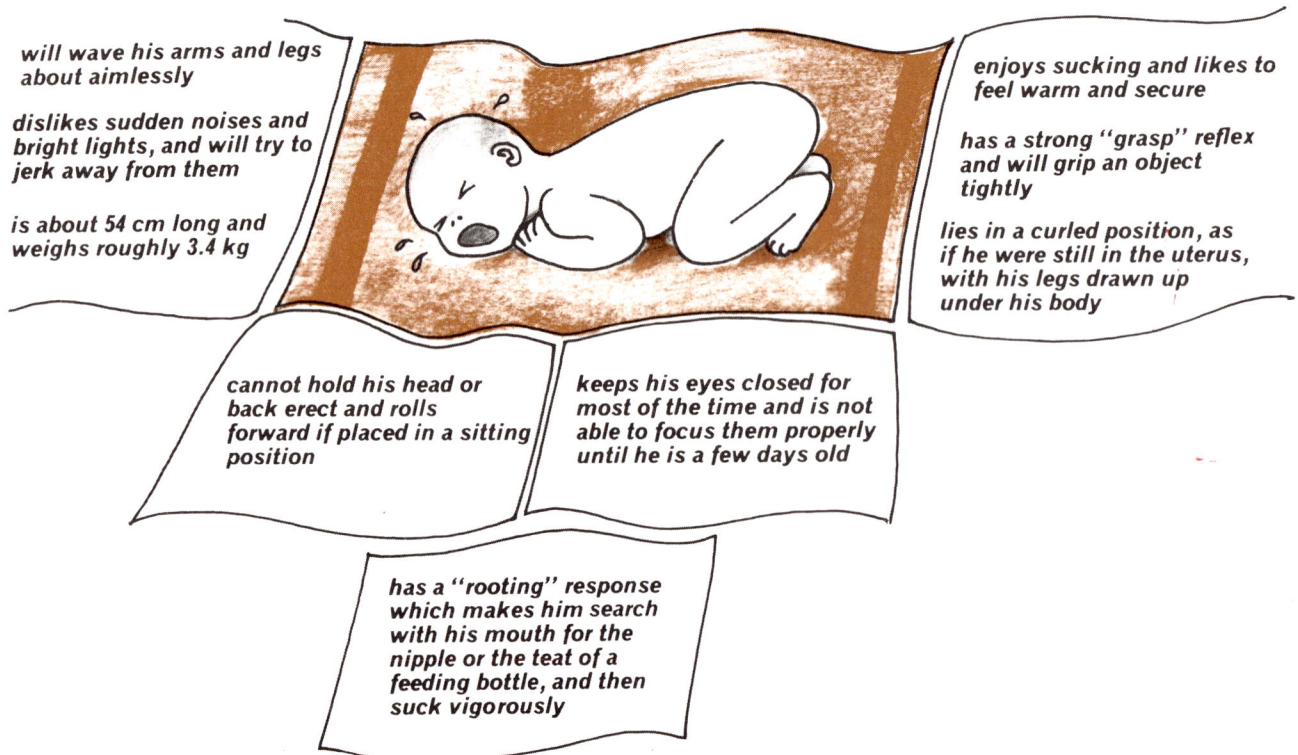

will wave his arms and legs about aimlessly

dislikes sudden noises and bright lights, and will try to jerk away from them

is about 54 cm long and weighs roughly 3.4 kg

enjoys sucking and likes to feel warm and secure

has a strong "grasp" reflex and will grip an object tightly

lies in a curled position, as if he were still in the uterus, with his legs drawn up under his body

cannot hold his head or back erect and rolls forward if placed in a sitting position

keeps his eyes closed for most of the time and is not able to focus them properly until he is a few days old

has a "rooting" response which makes him search with his mouth for the nipple or the teat of a feeding bottle, and then suck vigorously

Gradually, a baby's muscles become stronger and he is able to control the movements of his body. By the time he is three months old, a baby may have grown and developed sufficiently to be able to:

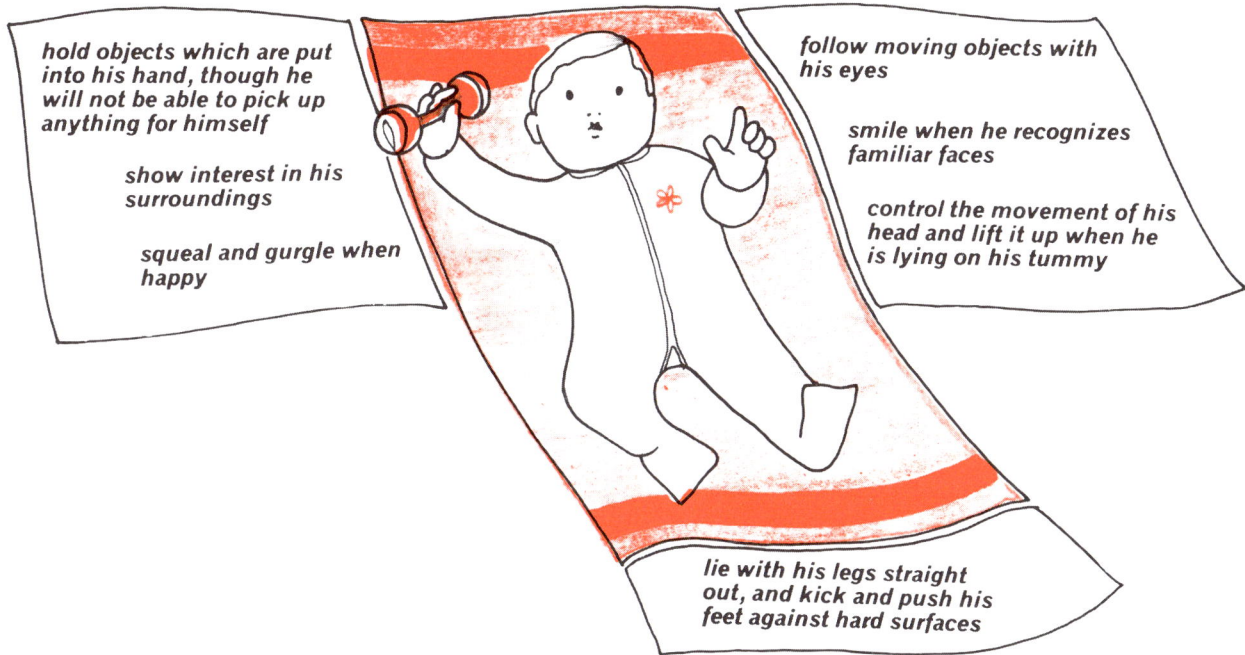

hold objects which are put into his hand, though he will not be able to pick up anything for himself

show interest in his surroundings

squeal and gurgle when happy

follow moving objects with his eyes

smile when he recognizes familiar faces

control the movement of his head and lift it up when he is lying on his tummy

lie with his legs straight out, and kick and push his feet against hard surfaces

At six months a baby will have doubled his birth weight and have gained more control over his body. He can sit up with support, and roll and wriggle on his tummy. He can reach for toys, grasping them firmly in his hand. Around this time his first teeth begin to break through and he starts to suck on toys with his hardening gums. He becomes more mobile as he grows and may be crawling at nine months. At this age he may have around four teeth.

At a year old he will be pulling himself up on pieces of furniture and may be standing unaided for a short while. When he begins to walk, his legs are wide apart for balance and he walks with a jerky, ungainly appearance. Around this age he can pick up and drop small objects, and will happily throw his toys out of his pram or cot.

At eighteen months a baby can usually walk fairly well with his feet closely together. He can pull, push and carry toys around, and bend down to pick up objects. His balance is good. This is the period of exploration and discovery. He will climb on to chairs, clamber over furniture, explore cupboards, empty book shelves and crawl up and down steps. He will follow his parents about the house trying to copy their actions.

By two years he can usually trot or run with confidence but may still have difficulty in stopping. A young child has a full set of teeth (20) by the time he is two and a half. He has control over his bowels, and will be dry during the day-time.

At three years a child can run, hop, jump, balance on one foot, climb and throw a ball. He can build a tower of bricks and draw definite shapes such as lines and circles. He can dress and undress himself and will attempt to undo and fasten buttons. A three-year-old will usually sleep for around 12 hours each night.

Opposite is a guide to show the various stages of mental and muscular development in the first three years of a baby's life.

The development of language

Early attempts at speech will take the form of cooing and gurgling, and a baby of five to six months is capable of showing pleasure and displeasure by laughing and crying. He can communicate feelings such as anger, pain, hunger, frustration and tiredness by using different expressions of crying, and he is capable of understanding and recognizing some words, even though he cannot say them himself. This is a child's passive vocabulary. During the development of language skills, the passive vocabulary is always more extensive than the active or spoken vocabulary. Usually the word "no" can be clearly understood at six months old, and first attempts at "Da-da" and "Ma-ma" can be detected from nine to ten months. Most children will have spoken their first words by twenty months. The average one-year-old will have an active vocabulary of two to three words, and can imitate many sounds and signals, e.g. waving "goodbye".

A two-year-old can have a vocabulary of about two hundred words, and may be forming quite complicated

Range of time when acquisition of skill can be expected	Skill
Around 3 months	Learning to control the movement of the head. Smiling and recognizing faces. Holding objects given to him.
6 to 8 months	Sitting upright without support.
8 to 12 months	Pulling himself up to a standing position.
9 to 12 months	Pulling himself along the floor on his bottom or crawling.
11 to 18 months	Beginning to walk unaided.
12 to 15 months	Holding and drinking from a cup.
15 to 18 months	Putting one block on top of another to build towers. Using a spoon to feed himself.
17 months to 2 years	Walking confidently and climbing up and down stairs.
18 months to 2 years	Kicking a ball.
2 to 3 years	Balancing on one foot. Drawing definite shapes such as lines and circles. Undressing himself and putting on items of clothing; attempting to undo and fasten buttons.
Around 3 years	Building a tower of blocks.

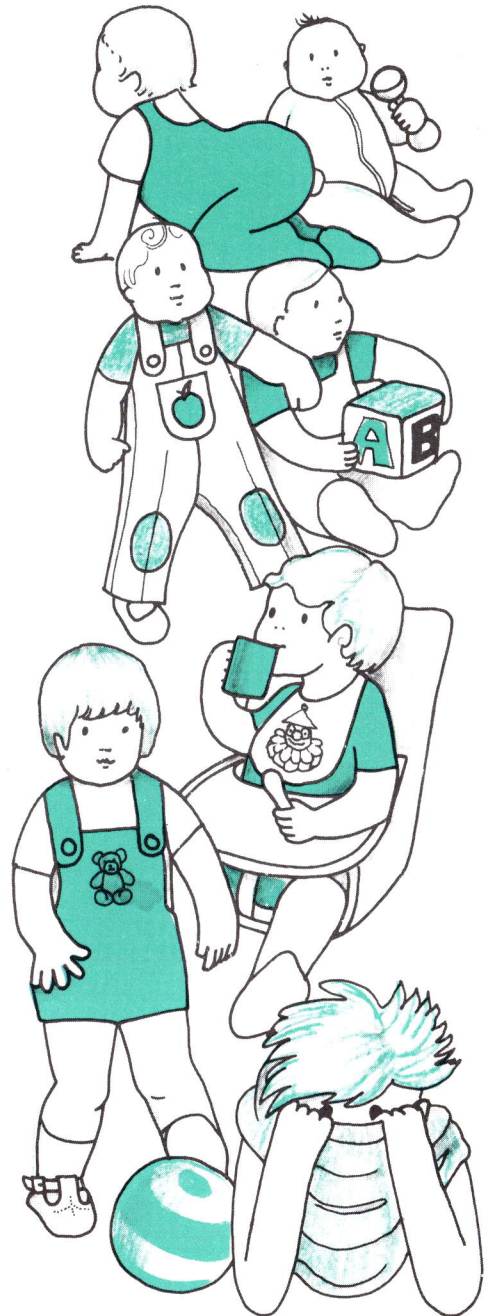

sentences. By the end of the third year, his active vocabulary may have grown to about eight to nine hundred words.

A child usually learns the different parts of speech in this order:

1 Interjections e.g. "No", "hot";

2 Nouns e.g. names of people, toys, parts of the body, articles of clothing, pieces of furniture, utensils such as cup and spoon, colours;

3 Adjectives e.g. good, lovely, nice;

4 Verbs e.g. "doing" words, such as eat, drink, play, count, draw, touch, sing, wave, clap, smile;

5 Adverbs, prepositions and *conjunctions* come later.

A child's language development will be affected by:

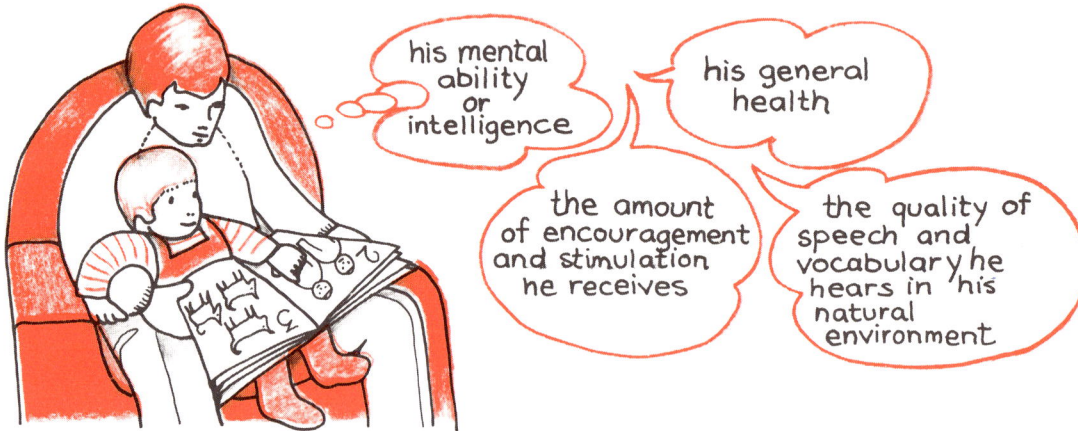

his mental ability or intelligence

his general health

the amount of encouragement and stimulation he receives

the quality of speech and vocabulary he hears in his natural environment

Here are some ways in which parents and adults can help a child in his speech development.

1 Talk to a child continually. This introduces the tiny baby to the rhythm of speech and gives the older child sounds to copy.

2 Always speak slowly and clearly.

3 Form short, simple sentences which are easily understood.

4 Encourage a child to speak to you. Listen carefully and always answer any questions.

5 Be patient when he is faltering over words and do not interrupt to finish off sentences for him.

6 Try not to show concern over stammering, mispronunciations and slurring of speech, and do not continually correct his mistakes.

7 Use words which are easily understood but do avoid "baby talk". This type of language has eventually to be unlearned, a stage which can be confusing to a young child.
8 Introduce a child to the magic of nursery rhymes. These can be sung, narrated, read together, made into finger action plays or turned into games.
9 Have a regular storytime session and talk about any colourful pictures.
10 Introduce new words to develop a wider vocabulary and use repetition as a means of helping a child to memorize.
11 Watch suitable nursery or pre-school television programmes together, or listen to nursery records.
12 Continually praise and encourage a child's progress. A loving, caring atmosphere encourages learning.

Emotional and social development

From birth, a baby experiences strong bodily sensations associated with pain, hunger, heat, cold, the movements of his muscles and the need to empty his bowels. If he feels frustrated, uncomfortable or in pain, his reaction is one of anger, and he will cry, scream or kick in rage. This feeling of anger quickly turns to love and affection, when his discomfort is removed or his desire has been satisfied. This is illustrated when a baby strokes, caresses and smiles at the person who feeds him, the one who satisfies his hunger.

A new-born baby likes to feel warm, secure and comfortable. If he is startled by sudden loud noises or rough handling, he becomes disturbed and restless. He stiffens, throws out his arms and cries. He likes to be left undisturbed with a blanket tucked snugly round him for warmth and security. When awake, he enjoys listening to a soft voice and being rocked gently. By the age of three months, he smiles and shows pleasure by wriggling about and stretching. He becomes excited when his mother or father talks to him, and gurgles when being cuddled. He lies awake for longer periods of time, contentedly watching people's movements. When uncomfortable or hungry, he cries crossly but will stop suddenly when he has his parents' attention.

As he grows older he becomes more interested in his surroundings and more responsive and alert. He still shows anger and annoyance by crying, screaming and kicking, but can often be easily distracted.

A young child is capable of strong feelings of jealousy. He does not want to share his parents' affection with other brothers, sisters or adults, and can clearly demonstrate this on the arrival of a new baby. Understanding parents can do much to prevent a young child from feeling jealous.

A baby's social development hinges on security. He needs to feel loved and part of a stable family unit. If a child is sure of his family's affection, he will be more willing to accept the company of other adults and children. A young child should be introduced gradually to new faces, preferably in the security of his own home. He is normally friendly but does not respond immediately to strangers.

When he is about six months old he may show willingness to play with a stranger, if one of his parents is near. From eighteen months onward he may play happily in the presence of other children, each intent on his own activity.

It is a good idea, around this time, for a parent to invite other young children round to play. In this way a young child can be encouraged to be sociable, and to make friends and play with children of his own age. From about three years onwards he may be introduced to nursery school or a local playgroup. At first he may cling and become very upset at the thought of leaving a parent, but with patience and understanding he will lose his shyness and sense of insecurity.

A young child's relationship with other children usually falls into three stages:

1 At first he will be completely indifferent to other children.

2 He may then become aggressive and push, pull or hit out at other children.

3 He will gradually accept other children and play happily with them.

The importance of play

A tiny baby learns by seeing, touching and hearing, so it is important to offer stimulation with as many sense-training toys as possible. When a baby is given a rattle, he will:

a look at it;

b touch it;

c listen to the sound it makes.

He will get enjoyment from listening to the rattle but he will also be learning by exploring the shape and feel of the rattle with his eyes, fingers and mouth. In this way he is learning about his environment. As he grows older his reactions will become sharper, and his natural curiosity about the world around him will increase. Wise parents will provide toys which stimulate a young child's senses and encourage him to explore his surroundings.

Here are some suitable toys for a baby.

UNDER 6 MONTHS
colourful, attractive rattles
mobiles
pram beads
teething rings
soft nursery animals
floating bath toys

6 TO 12 MONTHS
building and nesting beakers
washable cuddly vinyl toys
large balls
tambourine
play truck with plastic bricks
rubber hammer
plastic beakers
wooden spoons
Teddy bear
saucepans with lids
cotton reels

12 TO 18 MONTHS
interlocking building cubes
rag or board books
colourful picture books
hammer and pegs
rag doll
pull-along toys on wheels
musical toys such as drum, trumpet
abacus or beads on a string

A child's physical and mental development will be influenced greatly by his play. Play can help a child to:

a develop muscular skills, be physically active and learn to control his body;

b be creative and constructive;

c be imaginative and imitate adult situations;

d develop intellectually.

A child learns through play. The tiny baby explores his world with his mouth, eyes, ears and fingers, but as he grows older and more mobile, he investigates his environment with his hands and body. He becomes able to pull, push, drag, poke, drop, throw, open, close, empty, fill, tip, bang, build up, knock down, and squeeze the objects around him. Whilst doing these actions he is developing muscular skills. Play helps physical co-ordination so that a young child becomes able to crawl, sit up unaided, pull himself up, walk, climb, balance, jump, hop, and run. He is also learning how to handle materials. This improves his dexterity and helps his powers of sight and hearing.

Play encourages a child to communicate. The development of language is essential if a child is to convey his ideas to other people. At first a young child will play happily with or in the company of his parents or brothers and sisters, but then he will begin to play with friends of his own age. This will teach him to share his possessions and help him to overcome shyness and anti-social behaviour.

Creative work, such as drawing, painting, modelling, playing with sand, water, bricks and wood, helps a child achieve something. He gains personal satisfaction and pleasure from his own creation. He is able to express his feelings in his play, and give voice to his fears, delights and frustrations. Creative play also helps a child to develop self-control. At first he will not be able to concentrate on any one task for a long period of time but gradually he will learn that to create something worthwhile needs perseverance. He will become less careless and impatient, and be encouraged to exercise self-discipline.

Imaginative play, such as dressing up games, pretending to be other people, and all forms of drama, allows a child to have fun in a world of fantasy. It helps him to understand adult roles and situations, and how different people feel. He becomes aware of the responsibilities of parents, doctors, nurses, policemen, firemen etc., and is able to act out his own fears and anxieties, such as visiting the dentist, hearing his mother and father quarrelling or the loss of a treasured toy or possession. Imaginative play allows a child to express aggressive and violent feelings in a way that is not harmful.

This is a necessary and valuable outlet for his violent impulses.

Play can also stimulate interest and curiosity, and help a child to develop intellectually. Games which match sizes and shapes, e.g. jigsaw puzzles and posting boxes, help a child to develop an awareness of space, area, numbers and colours. They also encourage a child to reason, work out solutions to problems, collect facts and learn to think.

Play is therefore vitally important for the physical and mental development of a child. A wise parent will give:

a ample opportunities for long periods of play;

b help, encouragement and approval;

c the space, equipment and materials needed.

Some ideas for play equipment for a young child are given over the page.

Here are some points to remember when choosing play equipment.

1 Choose toys which are suitable for the age of the child.

2 Buy sturdy, well-made toys, which will last.

3 Always check that any paint, dye or lacquer is non-toxic.

4 Materials and fillings should be non-inflammable.

5 Check that there are no sharp edges that could cut, or pins and staples that could scratch.

6 Any folding mechanism should be childproof, and any clockwork mechanism should be completely enclosed.

7 Wheeled toys, such as trucks, scooters and tricycles, should be stable and easy to steer.

8 Soft toys should have screw-in eyes. Limbs of dolls should be securely attached.

9 Electric motors should not exceed 24 volts.

10 Look for toys which are recommended by the British Standards Institution and carry the Kitemark symbol.

11 Always remove the plastic covering bag or wrapper before letting a child play with a toy.

12 Large items of play equipment, such as a climbing frame, swing, see-saw and sand pit, should be checked regularly for stability and for any defects.

Remember. Water play should always be supervised. Never leave a paddling pool, washing machine, bath or sink full of water unattended.

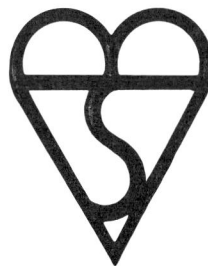

Play equipment for developing muscular skills	*Creative play equipment*	*Imaginative play equipment*	*Play equipment for intellectual development*
bead-threading kits	blackboard	brush and dustpan	abacus
boxing gloves	building bricks, blocks and straws	bubble-blowing kit	card games e.g. "Snap", "Happy Families"
climbing frame	chalks	cooking utensils	
commando net	clay	cowboys and indians play equipment	clock
football	constructional toys	dolls	colourful books
monkey rope	crayons	doll's house	dominoes
planks, boxes and barrels	dough	doll's pram	games which match sizes, shapes and colours
push and pull toys on wheels	dry foods e.g. lentils, pasta	dressing-up clothes	
rocking horse	empty boxes, rolls and cartons	fire station	hammer and pegs
roller skates		garage	jigsaw puzzles
rope ladder	glue	large cardboard boxes	mosaic sets
scooter	paint	model farm	musical toys
see-saw	paper and blunt-ended scissors	Noah's ark	nuts and bolts
sewing cards	Plasticene	nurses and doctors play equipment	peg board
skipping rope	sand	shop equipment	picture-tray puzzles
slide	scraps of material	small table and chairs	posting box
swing	toy tool kit	spade and bucket	
toboggan	water	telephone	
trapeze		toy cars, lorries, trains, aeroplanes	
tricycle		watering can	
trolley		Wendy house	
truck			
wheelbarrow			

Diet

Milk is the only food that a baby requires for the first three months of his life. Most brands of dried milk have vitamins and minerals added, so there is no need to supplement the milk diet with vitamin drops. A breast-fed baby though, or one who is fed with evaporated milk, **will** require added vitamins, and these can be obtained from a Child Health Centre. Vitamin drops can be mixed with a little milk or water, or given to a baby straight from a spoon. Rose hip syrup, orange or blackcurrant juices are all rich in vitamin C, and can be used to supplement a baby's milk diet, if necessary.

After about three months there may be signs that a baby requires some solid foods to satisfy his hunger. Mixed feeding should be introduced if a baby:

    a starts to suck his fists vigorously;
    b continues to wake up early for his next feed;
    c is fretful between meals.

Starting mixed feeding is called **weaning** a baby, and it consists of slowly introducing solid foods to supplement and then replace the milk diet.

When introducing mixed feeding:

    a use foods which are easy to digest;
    b only try one new food at a time;
    c make sure there are no lumps in the food;
    d continue with the normal milk diet.

Food for mixed feeding should be fine and free of all lumps. To prepare solid foods for a baby, use:

a sieve and wooden spoon	a baby mincer eg. the "mouli" type of food mill	a blender or liquidizer

Here are some suitable foods to use.

Cooked and puréed vegetables

Softly boiled egg yolk

Puréed fruit

Baby cereals

Puréed broths or home-made soups

Meat gravy (the sediment from a roasted joint)

Cheese flavoured milk sauces

Jellies, junkets, fruit fools, blancmange

The "mushy" variety of prepared baby foods (in tins, jars or packets)

These foods can be given on a teaspoon **before** the normal breast or bottle milk.

When a baby starts to enjoy mixed feeding:

  a gradually decrease the amount of milk;

  b gradually increase the solid food intake;

  c include daily vitamin drops;

  d offer cooled, boiled water between meals, when the baby is thirsty;

  e gradually introduce foods which are slightly harder to digest, and do not purée all the solid food, e.g. mince meat, mash vegetables, chop fish.

From approximately eight months onwards a baby should be eating a varied but well-balanced diet containing:

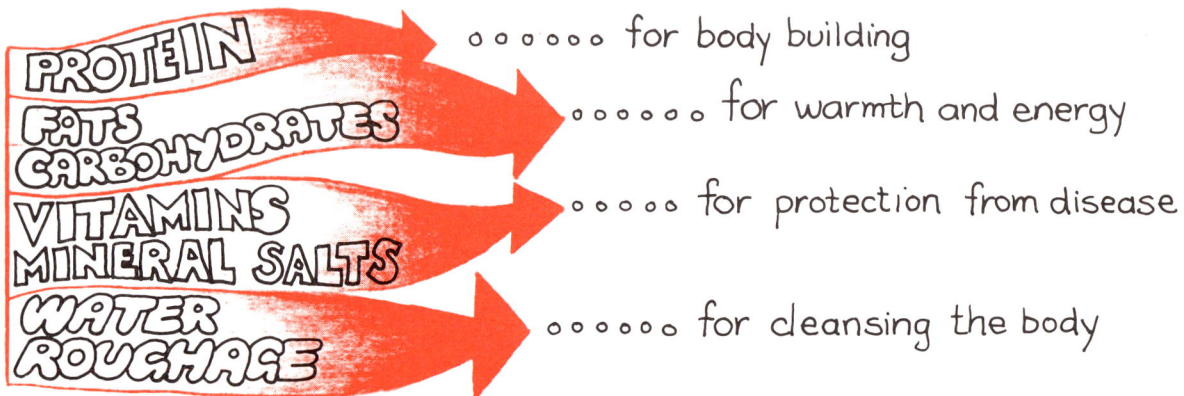

PROTEIN oooooo for body building

FATS CARBOHYDRATES oooooo for warmth and energy

VITAMINS MINERAL SALTS ooooo for protection from disease

WATER ROUGHAGE oooooo for cleansing the body

A normal varied diet will contain adequate supplies of each of these nutrients, but it is important that growing children receive plenty of these nutrients listed opposite.

Nutrient	Where found
Protein	Meat, milk, fish, eggs, cheese, pulse vegetables (peas, beans, lentils), cereals, new potatoes, nuts
Calcium	Milk, cheese, bread, eggs, green vegetables
Iron	Egg yolk, liver, kidney, meat, raisins, black treacle, bread, Brussels sprouts, spinach
Vitamins C and D	Fruits, vegetables Butter, eggs, milk, oily fish, cod liver oil, cheese

Here are some suitable foods to use from eight months onwards.
Boiled or scrambled egg
White fish
Beef, lamb, mutton, liver, chicken, turkey
A variety of cooked vegetables and fruits
Cottage cheese
Spaghetti, macaroni and rice
Yoghurt
Thin sandwiches
Fresh fruit, such as orange segments, mashed banana, peeled apple

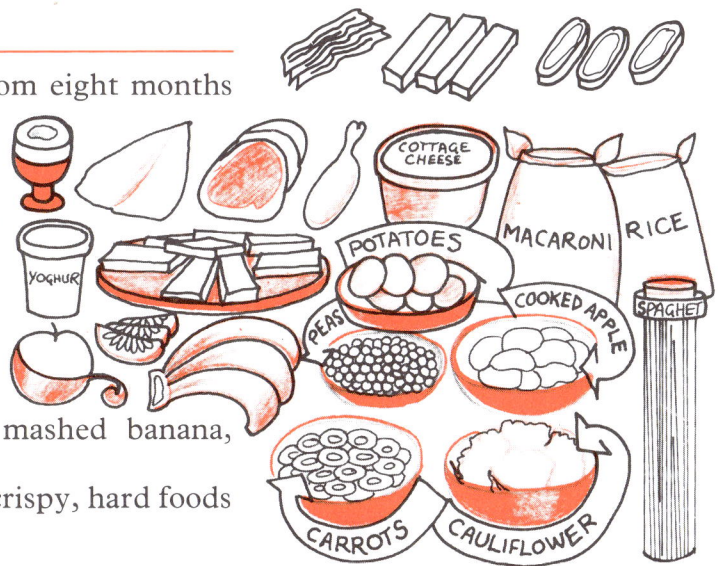

When a baby begins to cut teeth, some crispy, hard foods should be included in the diet e.g.:
crispy, grilled bacon;
fingers of toast or fried bread;
buttered rusks with honey or syrup.

Here are some foods which are unsuitable until a baby has been fully weaned.

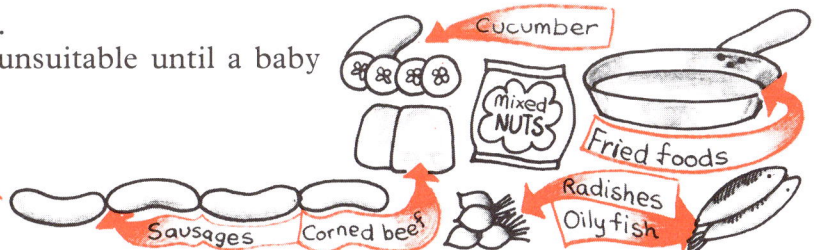

Do **not** give these foods to a tiny baby.

Around one year onwards, a baby will start eating the normal family meal, but the tougher foods should still be cut into small pieces or chopped roughly. He will also start to hold and drink from a cup by himself. The type with two handles and a raised spout is easiest for a baby to handle.

During the second year, a child will attempt to feed himself with a spoon. Meal times will then become slower and messier, but with patience a child will quickly master the art of being able to feed himself. He may acquire the skill to use a fork from two and a half years onwards.

A plastic plate with a suction base that stops it from sliding along the table, is useful when a child is learning to feed himself.

Here are some points to remember when feeding a toddler.

1 A meal should be colourful, attractive and varied in texture.

2 Gravies and sauces should be used to make food moist. Dry food can be unappetizing for a toddler.

3 Small helpings should be offered. They are less daunting for a young child.

4 Highly seasoned foods should be avoided, and salt and pepper used sparingly.

5 Meal times should be unhurried and peaceful occasions.

6 Children are entitled to have likes and dislikes, and should not be made to finish anything which they are not enjoying.

7 Nibbling in between meals should be discouraged.

Suction base

Foods to avoid between meals

Foods which can be allowed between meals if a child is hungry

Sleep

A new-born baby will sleep for most of the day, except for the periods when he is being bathed, changed and fed. As he grows older, he will sleep less, until, by the age of two, he may be sleeping for around twelve hours each night, with a short period of rest during the day. Sleep patterns will vary from child to child, and provided a child is happy and healthy, the amount of sleep he requires should not be a cause for worry.

It is a good idea to have a regular bedtime routine. This will help a child to settle down more quickly. Here are some points to remember when putting a child to bed.

1 A regular time for starting the bedtime ritual is helpful.

2 Try not to hurry a child or allow him to become excited. Bedtime is not the best time for playing violent or energetic games.

3 Wash and undress him quietly, then make him comfortable in his own bedroom.

4 A story, a quiet chat about the day's events or a lullaby can make bedtime a pleasant, relaxing occasion.

5 Always check that any favourite toys and familiar objects are nearby, before kissing a child goodnight.

6 If a child appears to settle more easily with a light, leave a small nursery lamp or landing light burning.

7 Do not rush to answer each small cry. Leave a child to settle down undisturbed.

8 If a child has difficulty in getting to sleep:

    a leave out the early afternoon rest;

    b give him a hot, sweet milk drink just before bedtime;

    c let him look at a picture book after you have kissed him goodnight.

Hygiene

Cleanliness is vital for good health, and the basic rules of hygiene should be taught to a child from a very early age.

Regular washing:

    a removes dirt and sweat;

    b keeps the skin clean and fresh;

    c keeps the pores open and helps to prevent spots, blackheads and other skin complaints;

d prevents stale and unpleasant smells;

e helps to prevent the spread of disease.

It is important that parents set an example and have good hygiene habits themselves, so that a child can imitate their behaviour. A child will quickly notice if his parents wash their hands before each meal and whenever they have been to the lavatory, and will want to copy them.

A tiny baby should be bathed daily, and his buttocks cleaned at each nappy change. The toddler should have a bath or shower, or be stripped and washed all over, once a day. Care should be taken to clean:

the neck and behind the ears

❁ under the arms

❁ the buttocks

❁ the hands and nails

❁ in between the legs

the knees

❁ the feet, especially around the ankles and in between the toes

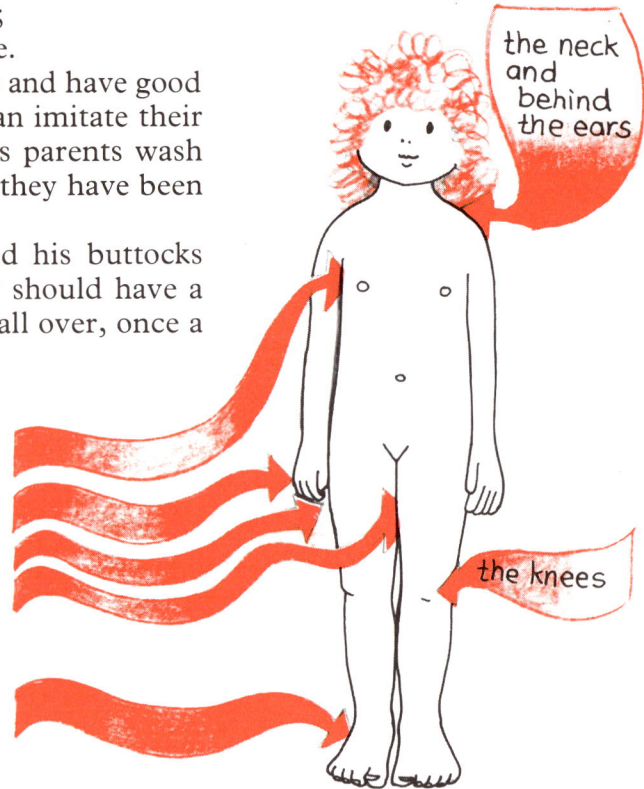

From an early age a child should be encouraged to wash himself, though parental supervision will be needed. A platform, upturned box or special step-stool placed in front of the wash-basin, will help to overcome the height problem.

Here are some other rules of hygiene which should be taught to a young child.

1 Hair should be brushed and combed each morning and evening, and be washed once a week.

2 Teeth should be brushed each morning, and last thing at night before going to bed.

3 Hands should be washed after every visit to the lavatory, and before each meal.

Control of the bladder and bowels

The age at which a child is able to control the working of his bladder and bowels, varies considerably. Usually bowel control develops before bladder control.

It is important that a child is able to develop bladder and bowel control in a relaxed, unhurried and happy atmosphere. He should not be forced to sit on the potty for long periods of time, or be scolded for accidents. Control will come gradually. Usually a child will have complete control over his bowel movements by the age of two and a half years, may be dry during the day by two years and dry during the night by three years.

Here are some points to remember when helping a child to gain bladder and bowel control.

1 It is pointless to expect a tiny baby to use a potty. This can only be an uncomfortable and upsetting experience. A young child can be introduced gradually to a potty in his second year, and should be encouraged (not forced) to use it after each meal and at regular intervals during the day. A sturdy potty that has a wide firm base should be used.

2 Encouragement and praise will help a child to gain control over his reflexes. He should not be punished, threatened or ridiculed when he is unsuccessful.

3 When a child begins to go to the lavatory, it is a good idea to use a trainer seat. This makes the lavatory pan look smaller and less frightening. A step-stool or platform will also be needed to help a child to climb on and off the lavatory.

4 It is not easy for a child to remove a nappy, so when a child is learning to use the potty or lavatory, it is more convenient to dress him in training pants. Training pants are made of terry towelling material. They are comfortable to wear, absorbent in the event of accidents, and can be easily pulled up and down.

5 A child can be encouraged to stay dry during the night by being:

    a put to bed without a nappy;

    b dressed in nightclothes which are easily and quickly removed;

    c given a potty at the side of the bed;

    d given nothing to drink after his tea-time meal.

Soft, absorbent terry towelling sheets are comfortable and easy to wash, and a rubber sheet placed under the ordinary sheet will protect the mattress during the toilet training process.

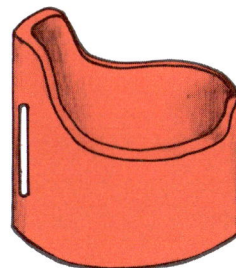

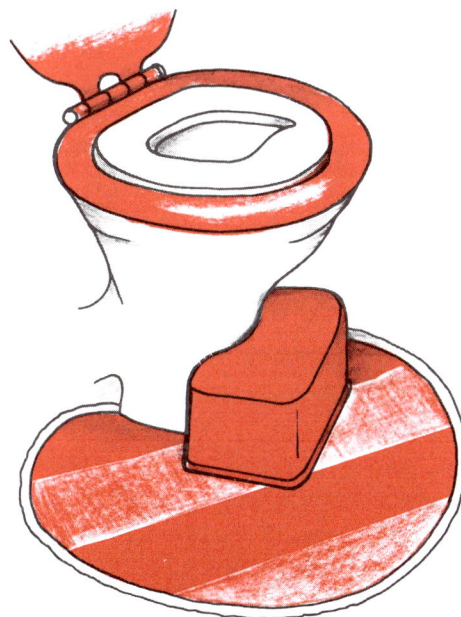

6 When a child is learning to control the bowels, his diet should contain plenty of roughage. This will make his stools regular and soft. If a child becomes constipated, his stools will be hard and he will find it painful. This could seriously interrupt the training process.

Think and Do

1. What advice would you give to a young couple, whose toddler is afraid of the dark and has difficulty in falling asleep at night?

2. Give *four* points to consider when planning meals for a toddler. Plan a day's meals for a young child who does not like fish or cheese.

3. What is meant by each of the following:
a. the "rooting" response of a new-born baby;
b. a child's passive vocabulary;
c. sense-training toys?

4. Give *four* basic rules of hygiene that a toddler should learn. Why is it important to wash frequently?

5. Find out the current prices of a potty, a toilet-training seat and a pair of training pants. How can a young child be helped to control his bladder and bowels?

6. Make a toy, game or book which would be suitable for a two-year-old. In your notebook, write a list of points which should be remembered when making, choosing and buying toys.

7. How can parents help a child to develop language skills?

8. Why is play important to a young child? Draw or describe *four* pieces of equipment that would help a toddler to develop muscular skills.

9. Explain what is meant by weaning a baby. List *four* foods which could be used when introducing mixed feeding. How should each of the foods by prepared?

10. In your notebook, write a paragraph describing the appearance and behaviour of a new-born baby.

The pre-school period (3 to 5 years)

The average three-year-old is no longer a dependent infant. He has slowly developed into an active, curious and mischievous individual who shows a remarkable degree of self-reliance.

Physical growth and development
An average child weighs:
about 14·5 kg at three years;

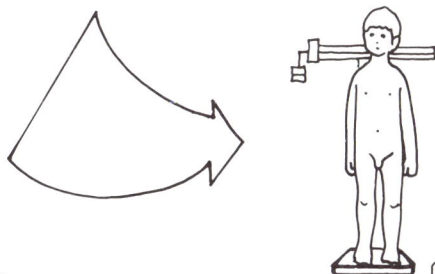

about 15 to 18 kg at four years;

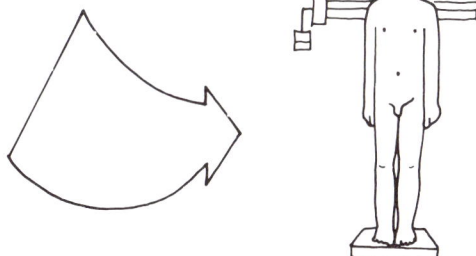

about 16 to 20 kg at five years.

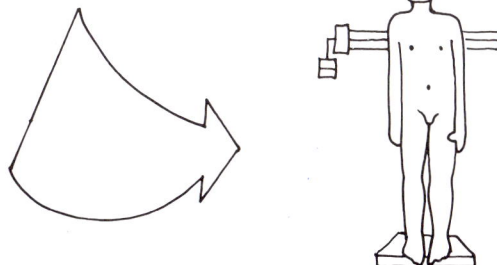

He measures:
about 93 cm at three years;

about 92 to 101 cm at four years;

about 102 to 110 cm at five years.

The development of muscular skills

Although the physical growth of the pre-school child has slowed down, there is rapid progress in the acquiring of mental and muscular skills.

An average three-year-old can run and jump with confidence. He can throw a ball, climb up and down stairs easily and is able to ride a tricycle. His drawings are still simple, but when painting with colours he is totally absorbed and uses wide sweeping movements of the brush. He can cut with a pair of scissors and delights in building with blocks and bricks. He may even be attempting to construct simple bridges.

At four years he is physically very agile and boisterous. He can climb trees, frames and rope ladders, and swing from a trapeze. His balance is good and he can hop on one foot and skip. He may attempt to skip with a rope but will not be very successful. By now he can dress and undress himself with ease, and may even be trying to tie shoe laces. His pictures of people are clearly recognizable and show the head, body, arms, legs and facial features.

An average five-year-old can skip with a rope, ride a bicycle with stabilizers and use a scooter. He can jump over a rope, bounce on a space-hopper and turn somersaults. He enjoys kicking and throwing a ball and may even be able to catch one. Playing a musical instrument, such as the drum, tambourine, cymbals and triangle, is an absorbing pastime, and the five-year-old delights in singing, dancing and listening to music. He can draw and paint people and objects, and can colour in an outlined shape. Dressing and undressing present no problems and a five-year-old can wash himself, clean his teeth, and brush and comb his hair. He is able to use a handkerchief properly when blowing his nose.

There is a guide over the page to show the various stages of mental and muscular development during the pre-school period.

The development of language

The pre-school child is usually keen to communicate. He will chatter continuously and ask question after question. This can become very wearing, but the sensible parent will encourage a child's natural curiosity and quest for knowledge, and will answer his questions patiently.

A child's vocabulary will be influenced by the type of conversation he hears in his natural environment. It is helpful if:

a the young child is included in the general family discussion;

b his questions are answered simply and sensibly;

c he is encouraged to talk to other children and adults;

d he is encouraged to speak slowly and in complete sentences;

e any mispronunciation is ignored, but the correct pronunciation is given slowly and clearly in a reply.

Range of time when acquisition of skill can be expected	Skill
Around 3 years	Running quickly. Climbing up and down stairs easily. Pedalling a tricycle. Going to the lavatory unaided. Drawing crude, but recognizable, pictures of "a man".
3 to 4 years	Dancing to music. Throwing a ball. Playing with a constructional toy.
Around 4 years	Dressing and undressing himself with ease. Playing with a skipping rope (not very successfully). Drawing pictures of "a man" which show head, body, arms, legs and facial features.
4 to 5 years	Playing and enjoying a musical instrument such as a drum, tambourine, cymbals or triangle. Blowing his nose properly.
Around 5 years	Counting to ten and matching a number to a series of objects. Tying shoe laces. Recognizing the primary colours, and crayoning or painting within an outlined shape. Washing himself and combing his hair.

An average three-year-old will have a wide active vocabulary and will be speaking fluently in complete sentences. He will be able to distinguish between the singular and the plural, and will be able to give his christian and surname when asked. In the fourth year he may be able to recall and recite his address and telephone number.

The parents of a pre-school child should try to foster an interest in books. This can be done by:

enrolling him at the local library and going with him regularly to choose new books

setting an example and reading avidly

showing him how to care for books and turn over the pages correctly

discussing pictures, stories etc. with the child

buying attractive and worthwhile books as birthday and Christmas presents

reading to a child every day

There are many suitable television programmes which the pre-school child will enjoy. These programmes can be entertaining and educational. They will certainly help to stimulate a child's curiosity and widen his vocabulary. Watching television should be an enjoyable and shared experience. The various programmes can then be discussed and used as a basis for future creative activity. Indiscriminate viewing should be discouraged at this age.

When a child starts to attend a playgroup, nursery or infant school, he may acquire a vocabulary of swear words. A child will not necessarily realize the meaning or significance of the bad language he is using, so it is wise not to over-react to this situation. A calm request not to use such an "impolite" word, followed by an explanation of its meaning, if possible, will be more effective.

These programmes can be entertaining and educational.

Social development

The pre-school child gradually becomes less dependent on his parents. By the age of four, a child will enjoy playing with other children, and will be willing to share his toys. His play will be co-operative, but friendships will be made and broken easily. This is an active period and the pre-school child has much to stimulate, interest and delight him. Activities tend to be short-lived, and the four to five-year-old lacks concentration and can easily be distracted, unless the activity is very absorbing.

Around the age of five, he will start to enjoy organized team games, and will delight in taking part in a shared activity, such as a percussion band. This is the age of successful childrens' birthday parties, when lively, musical games are enjoyed by all.

As a child grows up and becomes more independent, he begins to assert himself, and this may take the form of aggressive behaviour and bullying. It is important that parents should teach their pre-school child to be considerate and tolerant towards other children.

A five-year-old is usually full of self-confidence and will boast and show off to his friends, though he may be nervous of older children. He is able to control his emotions to a certain extent but will still cling to his parents when hurt, frightened or ill. He is co-operative and friendly, and enjoys playing with other children especially when involved in imaginative or constructive play. He loves to please his parents and teachers and will try hard to gain their approval.

The importance of play for the pre-school child

It must be remembered that a child learns through play. In chapter eight we saw how play helps a child to:

    a develop muscular skills;
    b be creative and constructive;
    c be imaginative;
    d develop intellectually.

For the pre-school child, play becomes a shared activity. He enjoys mixing with friends of his own age, and through play he learns how to get on with other children, how to understand and show consideration for their feelings, and how to control his own anti-social instincts. Social, imaginative play widens a child's vocabulary immensely, and allows him a valuable outlet for his emotions. For example, aggressive feelings can be exhibited in "war" activities; gentle, protective instincts can be displayed in "family" games; real-life fears and anxieties can be enacted in plays, dressing-up games, the play house, toy hospital and shop.

A greater confidence in his own body control and balance, makes active play popular with the pre-school child. All types of climbing equipment can be used to give scope for active, imaginative play. Climbing frames, rope ladders, tree houses, swings and an assortment of planks, boxes and barrels will help improve muscular co-ordination and develop dexterity of movement.

Messy activities are needed at this age. Painting, modelling, papier mâché work, sand and water play will keep the pre-school child happy and absorbed for a long time.

Finger paints are popular, and can be used on paper or any flat surface that is washable, e.g. Formica, polythene sheeting or a metal tray. (Remember that for all kinds of artwork, plain shelf paper and rolls of lining wallpaper are much cheaper than good quality art paper.)

Finger painting is an absorbing pastime for the pre-school child.

Finger paints can be bought already prepared, or can be made by mixing thick powder paint with polycel, washing-up liquid, starch or cold water paste.

The pre-school child loves to scribble and this urge to draw should be encouraged.

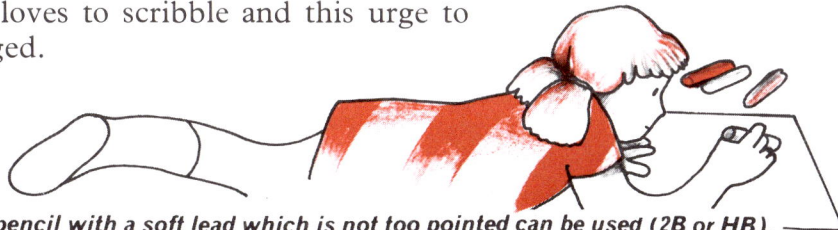

A good quality pencil with a soft lead which is not too pointed can be used (2B or HB).
Big, chunky wax crayons which are easy to hold, are very suitable for this age range.
Thick magic-markers can be very satisfying to scribble with, but supervision may be needed.
White and coloured chalks can be used on paper or on non-greasy blackboard surfaces.
Charcoal is an exciting medium to use.

A good, cheap modelling medium can be prepared by mixing three parts flour to one part salt and then adding cold water. (Self-raising flour gives a stretchy, springy paste that can be pulled into shape. Plain flour gives a pliable, less elastic dough that is good for modelling.)

Baking is an enjoyable pastime that can help the pre-school child understand the importance of number. Weighing and measuring the ingredients can be just as absorbing as actually making the dish. If the finished product is tasted and praised by the rest of the family, a child will be encouraged and stimulated to further successes.

The pre-school child will delight in constructional toys. These can range from simple bricks and blocks, which can be used to create roadway systems, garages, castles, houses etc., to the more expensive constructional toys, such as, Lego, Meccano, Construct-o-straws and Sticklebricks. Manual dexterity can be improved with jigsaw puzzles, mechanical toys, educational toys, dolls and action people that require dressing and manipulating.

At this age a child likes to collect objects. He is not very discriminating, and his collections can range from shells, conkers and fir cones, to stones, bits of paper and dead leaves. It is a good idea to start a nature table, so that all these precious items can be kept together. Curiosity about nature can be stimulated by such simple activities as:

a growing mustard and cress from seeds;
b growing "vegetable" flowers by placing the tops of carrots and parsnips on a saucer of water and watching the foliage appear;
c collecting caterpillars or frog spawn;
d looking after a goldfish.

The pre-school child will enjoy playing with kitchen "junk", such as discarded egg boxes, paper plates, empty packets, pieces of aluminium foil, toilet roll centres and old washing-up bottles. These can be used to stimulate creative play and to aid manual dexterity.

A good strong glue will be needed. This can be put into a shallow container, such as a plastic egg box, and used with a plastic or wooden spreader. Suitable glues are: Marvin Medium; Gloy Multiglue; Rowneys P.V.A. Small pre-cut

pieces of Sellotape can be used. This can be expensive but it provides a young child with a different and exciting way of sticking surfaces together. The pre-school child delights in making mosaics and collages. Seeds, pasta shapes, wood shavings, bits of wool and scraps of material will provide different textures and effects.

Diet

A young child should continue to eat a well-balanced diet. It is important that he has some of the following each day:

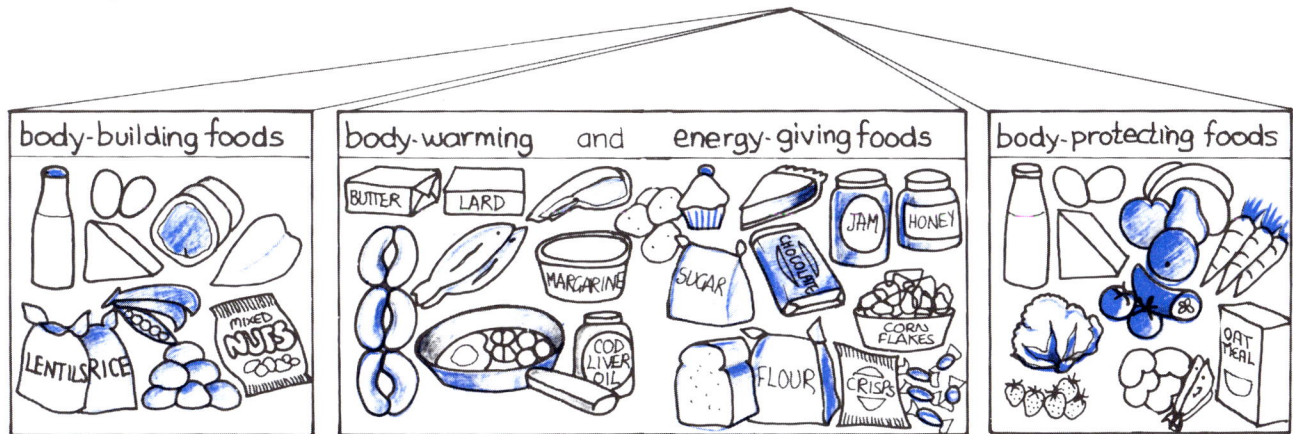

body-building foods | **body-warming and energy-giving foods** | **body-protecting foods**

The amount of food that a pre-school child requires will vary considerably, and so long as a child is growing well and has plenty of energy, this should not be a cause for worry. If a child is hungry, he will eat.

Meal times can often become scenes of confrontation, with a child asserting his newly found independence by refusing to eat. This is a normal phase for a pre-school child and is best ignored. As soon as he realizes that his rebellion against parental authority has failed, he will stop refusing food.

Around this age food fads may develop. One week a child will love a particular food, and then, just as quickly, he will develop a positive dislike for it. A wise parent will be patient and tolerant, and not force a child to finish his meal. Healthy eating habits should be encouraged by a good example. If a child sees that his parents enjoy their food and eat normal well-balanced meals, he will soon want to imitate them.

Here are some points to remember when planning meals for a pre-school child.

1 Try to plan varied, colourful and attractive meals.

2 Serve small helpings that are not overwhelming for a child.

3 Encourage a child to eat, but do not force him.

4 Have regular meal times and try to make them relaxed and pleasant family occasions.

5 If a child dislikes a particular food, serve an alternative. A green salad can be prepared instead of an unpopular cooked vegetable. If fresh fruit is not liked, then vitamin C can be included in the diet by having fruit drinks. If plain milk is unacceptable, then turn it into a blancmange, milk pudding, white sauce, egg custard or milk shake.

6 Do not allow a child to have an excess of carbohydrates. Too many cakes, biscuits, crisps and chipped potatoes may be popular, but they can lead to obesity in a child and health problems in later life.

7 Discourage nibbling in between meals.

Day care and pre-school education

Facilities for the social welfare and education of the pre-school child are provided by:

| day nurseries | nursery classes | nursery schools | playgroups | child minders |

Day nurseries are provided by the Social Services Department of a local authority. They take children from six months to five years of age. They are open for a full working day, so that children of working parents and one-parent families can attend. Priority is given to children with special needs.

Day nurseries are open throughout the school holidays. They are run by a matron and N.N.E.B. (National Nursery Examination Board) trained nursery nurses. Some day nurseries are becoming family day care centres, and are caring for the social welfare of the whole family.

Nursery classes are attached to primary schools, and cater for the needs of children between the ages of three and five. The school day is divided into two sessions – morning and afternoon. Most children are enrolled for one session only, attending nursery class in a part-time capacity.

A nursery class can join with the main school for assemblies, sports days etc., and this means that children become familiar with the school surroundings and routine, before they actually begin their full-time education.

A nursery class is run by a nursery teacher, helped by N.N.E.B. trained assistants.

Nursery schools are specially designed for the education of children between the ages of two and five. They are run by a head teacher and N.N.E.B. trained nursery assistants.

Playgroups are usually voluntary associations run by groups of mothers. Playgroups provide for the social, physical and educational development of children between the ages of two and a half and five.

Most playgroups rely on the active support and involvement of parents, and the mothers concerned with the day to day running of the groups benefit from the stimulation and companionship offered, and from an enriched parent-child relationship.

Playgroups must be registered with the Social Services Department, who in turn can pay for places for children in need. Playgroup leaders are expected to have completed a course of training.

Child minders look after other people's pre-school children during the daytime. Child minders use their own homes and have to be registered with the Social Services Department, who can supervise and inspect the premises, whenever necessary. Registered child minders charge for their services.

A child who attends a day nursery, nursery class, nursery school or playgroup, will benefit from being with other

children. He will learn to socialize and co-operate with other people, adults included. He will be surrounded by space, stimulation and play materials, giving endless scope for creative activities. Because everything is learned through play, he will come to associate learning with pleasure.

How to prepare a child for nursery and infant school
A sensible parent can help a child prepare for starting school by:

a encouraging him to be independent;
b teaching him to dress and undress himself;
c making certain that he can go to the lavatory by himself;
d encouraging him to enjoy books;
e talking, listening and playing with him;
f teaching him road safety;
g making him familiar with the school and the route;
h training him to use a handkerchief properly;
i teaching him to write and recognize his own name;
j checking that he has plenty of sleep each night;
k encouraging him to play with other children.

How to help a child mix with other children
There are many forms of organized activities for the pre-school child. A sensible parent will help a child to mix with other children by taking him along to a:

parent and toddler group

one o'clock club

Sunday school

local branch of the Tufty club

local theatre "workshop" for young children

crèche attached to a shopping centre

toddlers' gym or dance class

library-based story and activity session for the under-fives

A child can be encouraged to meet other children, on an informal basis, by being taken to a:

local park, playground or playing field

paddling pool or teaching pool in the local swimming baths

friend's house to meet other pre-school children

A few hints on baby-sitting

If you are asked to look after a baby or young child, remember that you are responsible for his safety, until the return of his parents. This is a serious and trusted position and should not be undertaken lightly. Always check that you know:

a where the parents can be contacted in an emergency (write down the address and telephone number);
b the telephone number of the family doctor;
c how to dial 999 (in the event of fire);
d if, when and how to feed the child;
e whether or not you are to bath him;
f at what time you should put him to bed;
g whether or not he has to be given any medicines.

A good baby-sitter, will also:

a keep the television, radio or record player turned low so that the child can be heard if he cries;
b check periodically that he is alright;
c keep the house neat and tidy;
d wash up after a supper snack or drink.

When a child has difficulty in getting to sleep:

a reassure him that his mummy and daddy will be back soon;
b offer him a drink of water;

   c remake his bed;

   d take him to the lavatory;

   e tuck him in with a covered hot water bottle, if he does not feel too hot;

   f tell or read him a short story;

   g kiss him goodnight and leave him.

If a child is still restless and cannot settle:

   a give him a warm drink of sweet milk;

   b leave the bedroom light on and let him look at a book or play with a toy.

Nightmares can be very frightening, and if a child wakes up screaming and shouting, he should be comforted at once. If he is old enough to explain his fears, he may try to talk about them, and this can have a calming effect. When he is ready to go back to sleep:

   a leave the bedroom door open, so that he does not feel so lonely;

   b switch on the landing light or a small nursery lamp, so that the bedroom looks warm and cosy.

Some other childhood problems

Temper tantrums. A temper tantrum can develop whenever there is a clash of will between a parent and young child. If a child feels thwarted and rebellious, he will start crying, screaming and kicking. He may even stop breathing for a short while and become blue in the face. This is called a "breath-holding" attack.

A temper tantrum should be ignored if possible. A child who is having a breath-holding attack should be laid gently on the floor. A parent should remain calm and unruffled. When a temper tantrum is not creating the desired effect, a child will quickly recover his temper. Then is the time to cuddle and reassure a child that he is still loved. With experience, a temper tantrum can often be anticipated and prevented by:

   a distracting a child;

   b using gentle persuasion;

   c retaining a sense of humour.

Jealousy. A young child can become jealous of any member of his family, but he feels particularly threatened by the arrival of a new baby. The powerful emotion he feels may be displayed as:

a anger and defiance;

b a refusal to eat his meals;

c a temporary regression in his development (i.e. he may temporarily lose control over his bladder and bowels, and resort to babyish behaviour);

d attention-seeking devices.

Wise parents will try to help a young child accept the birth of a baby brother or sister by:

a including him in all the preparations;

b letting him hold and play with the baby;

c encouraging him to help look after the baby;

d giving him extra love and attention;

e being understanding and patient with his regressive behaviour.

Lying and stealing. A child will lie when he is afraid of the consequences of his actions. He may feel insecure and frightened that he will lose his parents' affections, or he may fear physical punishment. Lying is a way of blocking out unpleasantness and taking refuge in a world of fantasy.

A child who continually lies may need to be reassured that he is loved. It is helpful to praise a child when he has owned up to a wrongdoing. This should not excuse the offence but will help to teach a child that truthfulness is important. Wise parents will try to set an example by being considerate and honest in their own actions.

Stealing may be a sign that a child feels unloved and is seeking attention or it may simply mean that a child does not appreciate the notion of ownership. A calm, understanding approach to this problem is more effective than a horrified over-reaction. A child should be told quietly that it is wrong to take another person's property and that he should return the object with an apology.

Planning a children's party

The success of a children's party depends on thorough planning and preparation. It is important to know, in advance, the number of guests who will be attending the party, so that a complete shopping list can be drawn up.

When compiling a shopping list, include all the items that will be needed. It is helpful to use the following headings:

1 Food and drink (always allow plenty to drink);

2 Tableware and accessories, e.g. paper or polythene tablecloth, paper or foil plates, cups, dishes, serviettes, plastic spoons, straws, paper hats, place cards, candles and cake decorations;

3 Party incidentals, e.g. balloons, prizes, wrapping paper, sweets, small take-home presents, giant box of paper tissues (useful for noses and spills).

The shopping and preparation of food should be done well in advance so that there is plenty of time, on the morning of the party, to:

a prepare the room by pushing back furniture and removing all small, breakable objects;

b arrange the table;

c blow up the balloons;

d plan and prepare the games;

e sort out the records, cassettes etc. that will be needed for musical games;

f wrap up the take-home presents and prizes;

g calm down an excited child.

Pre-school children enjoy lively, active games and a selection of the following is suitable.

LIST

FOOD:

TABLEWARE:

EXTRAS:

BALLOON-BURSTING TEAM GAMES

LUCY LOCKET LOST HER POCKET

HERE WE GO ROUND THE MULBERRY BUSH

MUSICAL- BUMPS CHAIRS PAPERS MATS

RING-A-RING-A-ROSES

ORANGES AND LEMONS

STATUES

FARMER'S IN THE DEN

THE HOKEY COKEY

A-HUNTING WE WILL GO

Try to include some quieter games that can be used to calm down the children when they get too excited. Here are some examples.

HUNT THE THIMBLE

PASS THE PARCEL

SIMPLE SIMON SAYS

PINNING THE TAIL ON THE DONKEY

When preparing food for a children's party, remember that young children like an assortment of small delicacies that they can nibble. Savouries are often more popular than fancy cakes, and a plentiful supply of crisps and small sausages are always appreciated. Here are some dishes which are suitable for a children's party.

Assorted sandwiches

Marmite
Peanut butter
Grated cheese
Egg
Meat paste
Salmon
Banana

Marmite

Egg

Salmon

Banana

Remove the crusts

Cut the sandwiches into small, attractive-looking shapes.
Rolls, pinwheels, and double-decker sandwiches are popular.

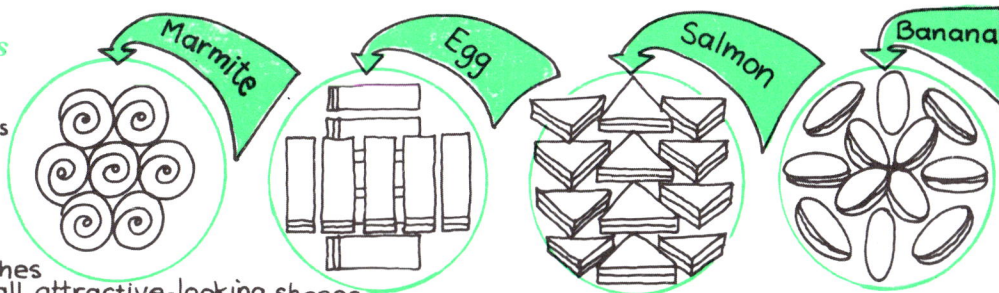

Savouries

Pieces of sausage, cheese and pickled onions
Small sausage rolls
Cheese straws
Assorted crisps and savoury biscuits
Marmite sticks
Pieces of celery filled with cream cheese

Make small, compact savouries which are easy to eat. Avoid using flaky pastry since young children find it difficult to handle.

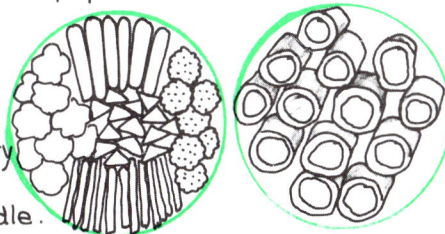

Cakes and biscuits

Small iced sponge cakes (use petits fours cases instead of bun cases)

Battenburg cake

Unfilled small meringues

Chocolate haystacks

Iced shortbread biscuits

Chocolate finger biscuits (on a hot summer's day, wafer or cream biscuits will be less messy)

Gingerbread men

Dessert (It is not wise to give a choice of more than two dishes.)

Jelly and ice cream

Fruit in jelly

Blancmange

Individual mousses or trifles

Slices of Arctic roll

Banana splits

Melon segments

Ice-cream sundaes

Birthday cake   A sponge cake, which is decorated with butter icing, chocolate drops or smarties is always popular. It can be baked and decorated in a novel shape, e.g. house, doll, train, ship, fort, rocket, book or zoo. The birthday cake is best kept until the end of the party, when the departing guests can be given a piece to take home, together with a small gift or tube of sweets.

Decorate cakes with Smarties, chocolate buttons, chocolate flakes, dolly-mixtures etc.

Serve the dessert in individual paper or foil dishes and do not forget to provide spoons.

Think and Do

1. How can sensible parents prepare a child for starting school?

2. List the day care and pre-school educational facilities which are available for the under fives. In your notebook, write a short paragraph describing the benefits of each one.

3. Say how you would deal with a child who:
a. is jealous of a new baby;
b. continually tells lies;
c. has temper tantrums;
d. uses bad language;
e. will not eat his meals.
4. Either make a toy, model, scrapbook or item of clothing, or write a short story for a pre-school child.
5. Make a list of suitable games for a five-year-old's birthday party. Plan the birthday tea and show how you would decorate the birthday cake.
6. Write a paragraph on each of the following:
a. television programmes for the pre-school child;
b. playgroups;
c. planning meals for the pre-school child.
7. Imagine that you are looking after a neighbour's pre-school child for a morning. How would you take care of the child? Suggest a suitable mid-morning snack and a lunch which you could easily prepare for the two of you.
8. List the points you consider important for a teenager to know before being left to baby-sit. How should a baby-sitter deal with a child who:
a. is unable to get to sleep;
b. is afraid of the dark;
c. has a nightmare?
9. How can parents help a pre-school child with the development of his language?
10. Copy the following diagram into your notebook. In each box, make a list of suitable items of play equipment.

PLAY EQUIPMENT FOR THE PRE-SCHOOL CHILD

For developing muscular skills, body control and balance	For imaginative play	For creative and constructive play	For intellectual development

The young schoolchild (5 to 7 years)

Physical growth and development

The growth rate of the young schoolchild decreases steadily.
An average child weighs:
about 16 to 20 kg at five years;

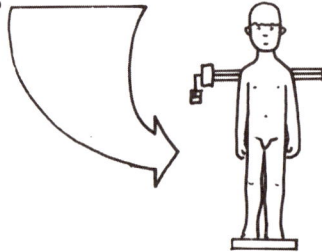

about 21 to 24 kg at six years;

about 22 to 26 kg at seven years.

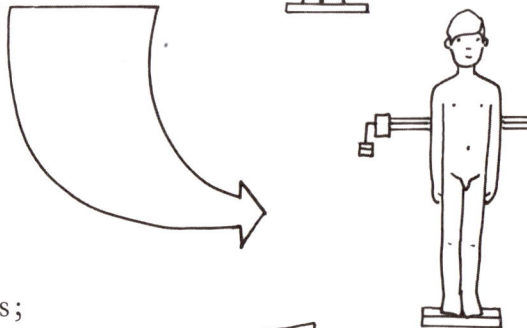

He measures:
about 102 to 110 cm at five years;

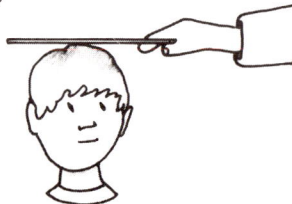

about 111 to 117 cm at six years;

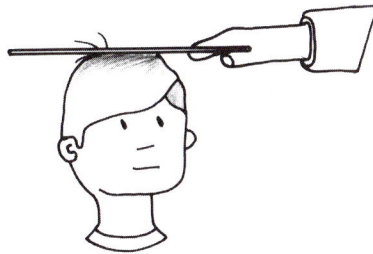

about 116 to 122 cm at seven years.

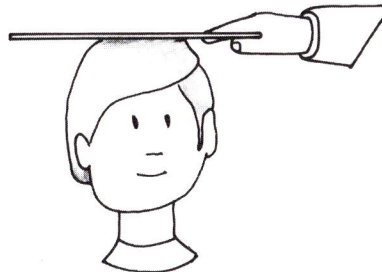

During this period there is little difference in growth rate between a boy and a girl, though a boy may be fractionally taller.

Mental development

In this country nursery or pre-school education is not compulsory, but when a child reaches the age of five, he is legally compelled to attend an infant school and start the first stage of his primary education.

The compulsory school age is reached at the beginning of the school term *following* a child's fifth birthday. For example, if a child is five in March, he should start school in April, at the beginning of the summer term. Many education authorities though, do accept a child for primary education at the *beginning* of the school term in which he has his fifth birthday, but this is dependent upon there being a vacancy in the reception class. A summer-born child may find that there is not a school place available, and he has to wait until September and the beginning of the autumn term before he can attend school. He may then be over five and a quarter years old, and will receive only two years infant education before being transferred to the junior school at the age of seven.

During the first years in the primary school, a child continues to learn through his senses. He needs to see, touch, smell, taste and hear things, to be able to understand what they are. He learns through his play to acquire the basic skills needed for reading, writing and number work. A normal young child is full of curiosity, and this can be a motivating force which helps him to learn.

There is a gradual growth in abstract reasoning. This develops slowly, as a child realizes that he can manipulate objects to solve practical problems. For example, a child will quickly learn how to fit differently shaped pieces into similarly shaped holes. This is the beginning of reasoning.

The young schoolchild shows a greater degree of concentration than the pre-school child, and is less easily distracted. Project work becomes absorbing and attention can be sustained over a period of time.

A child needs to repeat activities and it is by repetition that the learning processes develop, and the memory span increases.

A normal six-year-old is an active and energetic individual who can balance on boards, throw and catch a ball with ease, turn somersaults, run, jump, climb, skip with a rope and balance on roller skates. He delights in ball games and can kick a ball well and use a bat. He enjoys all physical activities including music and movement.

Milk teeth start to loosen and fall out around the age of six or seven, and the first permanent teeth begin to appear during this period.

By the age of seven a child can hold and manipulate small objects easily. This is demonstrated in a love for construction kits, such as Meccano, Lego and Sticklebricks and an interest in various handcrafts such as sewing, knitting and Plasticene modelling.

Social and emotional development

The young schoolchild shows a marked degree of independence and is usually a self-possessed and confident individual. He has more control over his emotions, than during the pre-school period, and is less likely to suffer from temper tantrums, jealousy and sulky displays of obstinacy.

His play is co-operative, and friendships are long-lasting and important. During the first years in primary school, there is little evidence of segregation between the sexes. A boy will play happily with a girl, and will share common interests and activities. Usually around the age of seven, a child will begin to show a preference for friends of the same sex, and groups or gangs may be formed. Jealousy and rivalry frequently arises between groups of children, and this allows the young schoolchild to exhibit aggressive and hostile feelings in a play situation.

The importance of play for the young schoolchild

The young schoolchild continues to learn through his play.

Muscular skills are improved by:
- ball games
- athletics
- bicycles, trucks and go-karts
- all types of climbing equipment
- roller skates, skate boards

Creativity can be encouraged by:
- carpentry
- painting
- cooking
- music
- gardening
- modelling in different mediums
- constructional toys
- puppet making, collage, papier mâché

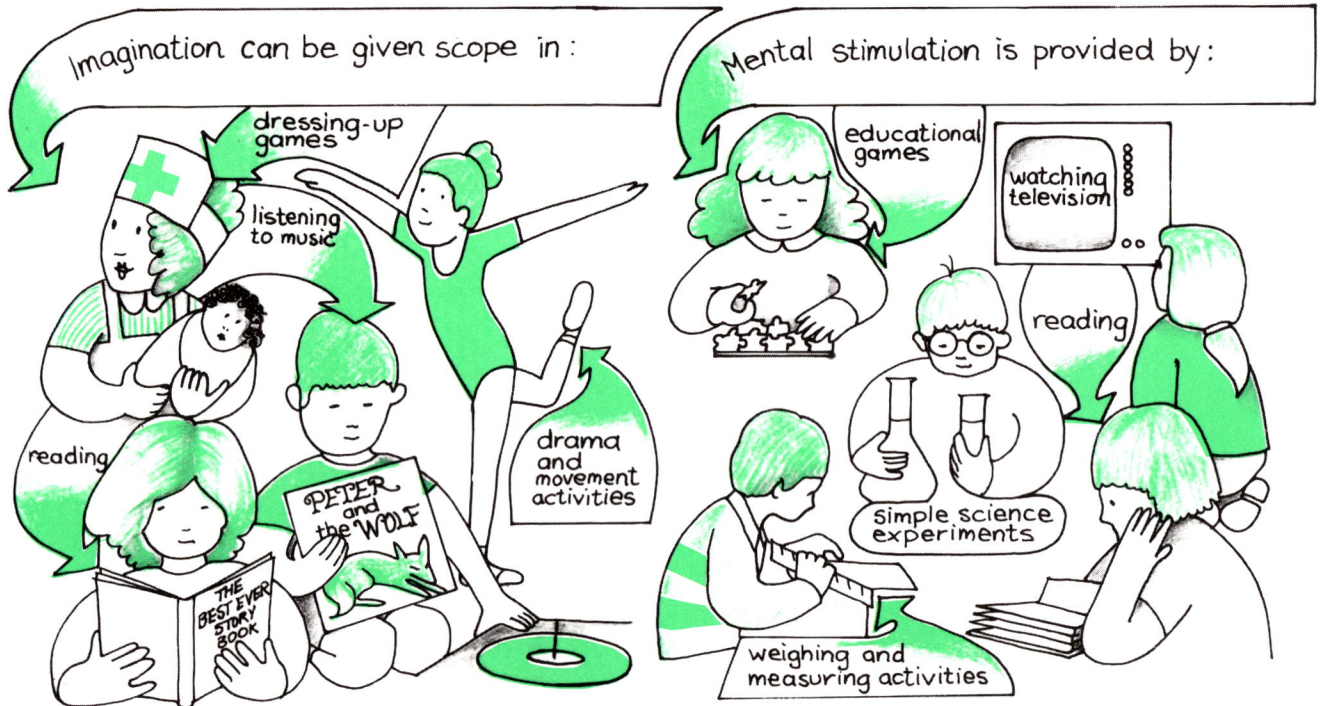

Imagination can be given scope in:
dressing-up games
listening to music
reading
drama and movement activities
PETER and the WOLF
THE BEST EVER STORY BOOK

Mental stimulation is provided by:
educational games
watching television
reading
simple science experiments
weighing and measuring activities

The young schoolchild will benefit tremendously from visits to local places of interest. These can range from a nearby post office, library, garage, fire station, supermarket, building site, canal, railway station and launderette to zoos, safari and adventure playparks, the seaside, the country, museums, art galleries and exhibitions. Visits, such as these, are important because they:

> *a* provide mental, creative and imaginative stimulation;
> *b* allow a child to explore a different environment;
> *c* give new ideas, information and knowledge.

Learning to read

By the time a child starts primary education, he will usually:

> *a* be able to speak;
> *b* be able to listen;
> *c* enjoy looking at books;
> *d* enjoy listening to stories;
> *e* have acquired a large active vocabulary.

These are all essential preparations for learning to read, and are referred to as signs of "reading readiness". During the first five years of a child's life, parents should actively try to encourage reading readiness by:

a fostering an interest in books and pictures;

b reading to him each day and following the printed words with a finger to accustom a child to reading from left to right;

c talking to a child slowly and in simple sentences;

d listening to a child and answering his questions;

e playing colour and shape matching games.

There are various methods of teaching reading, but most infant schools in this country use:

a the phonetic method;

b the look and say method;

c a combination of phonetic and look and say methods

d the Initial Teaching Alphabet (ita).

The phonetic method. With this method a child learns the sound of each letter, and the sounds made by particular combinations of letters. English is not a phonetically consistent language because some letters can be pronounced in different ways, and this can cause confusion. This method does help a child to build up an unfamiliar word.

The look and say method. With this method a child learns to recognize the complete shape of a word. Flash cards printed with simple words or sentences can be used daily to help a child remember word shapes, and build up a vocabulary of printed words which he recognizes.

The ita. This alphabet consists of 44 letters, each one representing a single sound. If a child is being taught to read using ita, his choice of reading matter can be limited unless ita books are provided at home and in the library.

Some children learn to read more quickly than others. A child's reading ability will be influenced by his:

The average child should be reading independently by the age of seven. When a child has learned to read independently for pleasure he should be encouraged to read as much and as often as possible. He will delight in reading aloud to his parents and showing off his newly acquired skill. Visits to the local library will provide an endless supply of books which will entertain and inform.

Here are some books which the young schoolchild will enjoy reading to himself.

Title	Author
Magic in my Pocket	Alison Uttley
Manxmouse	Paul Gallico
Fairy Gold	Joan Aiken
Three Bags Full	
The Little Ghost	
The Little Water-Sprite	Otfried Preussler
The Satanic Mill	
Lucky Dip	Ruth Ainsworth
Once, Twice, Thrice and Then Again	Dorothy Edwards
Next Time Stories	Donald Bisset

Here are some books which the young schoolchild will enjoy having read to him.

Title	Author
My Naughty Little Sister Books	Dorothy Edwards
Mrs Pepperpot Stories	Alfred Prøysen
Teddy Robinson Stories	Joan G. Robinson
Time for a Story	Eileen Colwell
Little Pete Stories	Leila Berg
Milly-Molly-Mandy Stories	Joyce Lankaster Brisley
Moomin Stories	Tove Jansson
Littlenose Stories	John Grant
The Wombles Stories	Elizabeth Beresford
Paddington Bear Stories	Michael Bond

Here are some books for the young schoolchild with a higher-than-average reading age.

Title	Author
The Robber Hotzenplotz	Otfried Preussler
Fantastic Mr Fox	
Charlie and the Chocolate Factory	Roald Dahl
James and the Giant Peach	
Lizzie Dripping Stories	
A Gift from Winklesea	Helen Cresswell
The Pie-Makers	
Doctor Dolittle Stories	Hugh Lofting
How the Whale Became	Ted Hughes
The Iron Man	

Diet

A young schoolchild eats less food than an adult, but requires a bigger proportion of body building and body protecting foods. He should have a well-balanced diet with adequate sources of:

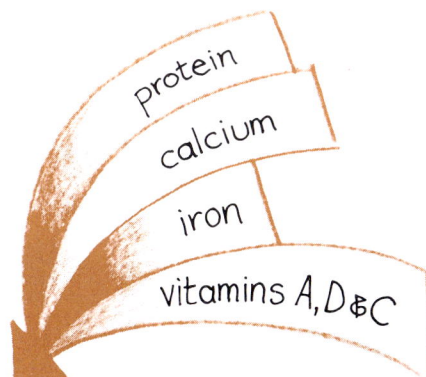

protein
calcium
iron
vitamins A, D & C

Energy-giving foods are also important but care should be taken to avoid an excess of carbohydrates which could cause weight problems.

Meals should be simple, attractive and varied in texture. Fatty foods and highly seasoned foods should be avoided.

At school a mid-day meal is available on each school day at approximately half the normal cost of such a meal. This meal should provide one third of a child's calorie and protein requirements for the day. Free milk is provided each day for all schoolchildren in infant schools. It is also made available to some children in junior schools, and to all handicapped children up to the age of sixteen.

Health education for the young schoolchild

Exercise. Regular exercise is essential for a growing child. Exercise:

    a helps the muscles to develop;
    b keeps the muscles firm and supple;
    c prevents constipation;
    d keeps the body alert, fit and healthy;
    e helps a child to sleep soundly at night;
    f gives him a healthy appetite;
    g quickens the beat of the heart and increases the supply of oxygen to the blood;
    h keeps the skin fresh by helping sweat to evaporate.

Cleanliness. A young child should be encouraged to form good habits in his personal hygiene. He should:

  a have a good wash first thing each morning and last thing at night (this should include the neck and behind the ears);

  b have a regular bath or shower;

  c brush his teeth twice a day and after eating sweet foods;

  d wash his hands before each meal;

  e wash his hands after going to the lavatory;

  f wash his hands after playing with any family pets;

  g brush his hair regularly and shampoo it about once a week.

Sleep. A young schoolchild needs 10 to 12 hours sleep each night. The bedroom should be cool and ventilated, and the bed should have a firm mattress that supports the body. Light, loose layers of bed coverings are better than thick, heavy blankets. A continental quilt is a suitable bed covering for a young child. It gives warmth without feeling heavy and does not restrict body movement.

Regular bedtime habits should be encouraged so that a young child knows at what time he is expected to go to bed. A warm drink of milk last thing at night will help to calm down an active child.

Care of the teeth. Teeth are formed before a baby is born. The first set of 20 teeth (milk teeth) usually start to appear between the ages of six months and two years. The permanent teeth (32 in a full set) start to appear later. A child should be:

  a encouraged to brush his teeth regularly each day and particularly *after* eating sweet foods;

  b taken to visit the dentist once every six months for a dental check-up;

  c encouraged to brush with a fluoride toothpaste *or* be given a fluoride tablet each day; (A dentist can also paint a fluoride preparation directly onto teeth to help prevent decay.)

  d discouraged from eating sweet or sugary foods;

  e given plenty of hard, crisp foods that need biting e.g. raw carrots, apples and celery.

TEETH SHOULD BE BRUSHED UP AND DOWN

A young schoolchild can be taught to floss his teeth using an unwaxed piece of dental floss. This helps to remove food particles and plaque from between the teeth.

Care of the feet. Toenails should always be cut straight across. Ingrowing toenails (an often painful condition) can result from toenails which have been cut down at the sides.

A child's feet should be checked frequently for verrucae (warts) and athletes' foot (a fungal infection between the toes). Verrucae can be treated by soaking the affected foot daily in formalin and then applying a special wart remover which can be obtained from a doctor. Athletes' foot can be prevented by careful drying between the toes and regular dustings with talcum powder. Special anti-fungal powders and ointments can be used.

A child's shoes should fit correctly in length and width. There should be room for growth. It is advisable to buy a child's shoes from a good shoe shop where trained assistants can measure each foot and suggest the type of fitting which is required. A sensible child's shoe gives support to a growing foot. It should have a low sturdy heel, and no ridges that could press down to cause deformities. Shoes should not be handed down from one child to another. Wellington boots, plimsolls and training shoes should be tried on before being bought.

It is equally important to check that socks and tights fit correctly. Stretch socks and tights should be big enough to prevent pressure on the foot.

Difficulties and problems with the young schoolchild

Bullying. This can be a means of showing frustration and lack of security. An aggressive and bullying child can be helped to regain his self-respect by being praised for his achievements and by being loved. Parents can help prevent bullying by:

    a encouraging a child to be considerate to other children;

    b helping to build up a child's self-confidence;

    c giving a child plenty of responsibility within the home and family;

d not using physical aggression in punishment;

e loving him.

If bullying becomes a problem to a child, either as the aggressor or the victim, his school should be prepared to help. If all else fails, a Child Guidance Officer, an educational psychologist, or an Education Welfare Officer can advise.

Insolence. This can be a way of showing tiredness, over-excitement or anxiety about a problem at home or at school. An understanding and sympathetic approach will often cure the condition. A child may need to talk about a secret worry and can then be helped to come to terms with it. Parents can help prevent this problem occurring by:

a always encouraging a child to behave politely to-wards other people;

b not being insolent, rude or churlish themselves;

c checking that a child is getting enough sleep;

d encouraging a child to discuss any problems that may be worrying him.

Shyness and timidity. A child who is shy and timid needs to be helped to gain self-confidence. He should be:

a encouraged to make friends and invite them home;

b praised for his achievements;

c encouraged to have a hobby.

A shy and timid child may be the result of over-excitable or over-timid parents, or he may be suffering from a feeling of inferiority brought on by his parents demanding too much of him.

Nail biting or thumb sucking. This is a very common problem for a young schoolchild. It may indicate nervous tension and stress, or it may simply be an indication of tiredness or boredom. A child may respond to a reassuring and sympathetic approach, but usually this habit will correct itself automatically with time.

An older child can be encouraged to take a pride in his personal appearance, and a nail file of his own may help. If thumb sucking persists when the permanent teeth have appeared, a doctor or dentist can be consulted.

The importance of music for the young schoolchild

Singing has always been part of a primary school curriculum.

Today the emphasis is on experimenting with sounds and enjoying music as a means of self-expression. Through music, a child can demonstrate his individual creativity.

Music can have a satisfying, soothing and therapeutic effect, and a child with a special handicap will often respond to the rhythm and feel of music.

Making music in the primary school can consist of:

a singing nursery rhymes, folk songs and modern songs from different countries;

b playing a musical instrument, such as the drum, tambourine, triangle, cymbal, glockenspiel, chime bars, recorder, castanets and xylophone;

c experimenting with sounds and making simple, home-made musical instruments;

d learning a little of the theory involved in reading music;

e listening to music;

f being given individual tuition by a music teacher.

A primary school in an immigrant community will often include the folk songs and musical traditions of the different immigrant races in its own particular area.

The role of the father in today's family system

The father in a family used to be considered the head of the household. He was often a stern figure whom the children seldom saw apart from at meal times. It was his duty to provide for his wife and family. His long hours at work meant that the responsibilities of bringing up the children were left to the wife.

In today's family system child-rearing is often shared by both parents. Though a mother will usually stay at home whilst a child is very young, there are many social and financial pressures which may tempt her back to work as soon as a child starts school, or even earlier. If the mother works, then the father should be prepared to share in the responsibilities of bringing up the children. He may:

take the children on visits to the local library

bath the children and help put them to bed

help with the family shopping

help with the household chores whenever possible e.g. lighting the fire, making the beds, cleaning the windows etc.

be prepared to stay in and baby-sit so that his wife can attend evening classes or relax with a favourite hobby

take the children out at the week-ends so that his wife can do any necessary housework

take turns with his wife in preparing family meals

help in the evening by playing with the children or reading to them

make time to attend P.T.A. meetings at the playgroup, nursery or school

If a husband is prepared to help his wife with the everyday problems of child-rearing, then there is a better chance that:

    a his wife will not be over-worked and harassed;

    b the marriage may be happier;

    c both husband and wife will have more time to spend together and with their children.

Nowadays the father may not be the only wage earner and provider in a family, but he is still a strong figure who stands for discipline and authority. A child respects his father and looks up to him for social and moral standards. If a father is an honest, loyal and caring person, then these attitudes of behaviour will be important to a child and will help to mould his character. A child will use his father as a model. A boy will try to copy his father's strength, skills and aptitudes, and a girl will be unconsciously influenced by her father's behaviour to his wife and family when she starts to look for a husband.

Think and Do

1. Imagine that you are meeting a neighbour's five-year-old daughter from school and looking after her until bedtime. Say how you would take care of the child and plan a suitable evening meal.

2. Choose **two** books which you think might be of interest to an average six-year-old. Read the books and write a short description of each one.

3. What is meant by the term "reading readiness"? Copy the following diagram into your notebook and write a suitable sentence in each of the boxes.

METHODS OF TEACHING READING

Phonetic	Look and say	Initial Teaching Alphabet

4. Plan a suitable menu for each of the following:

a. a birthday tea for a seven-year-old;

b. a picnic meal for a family outing to the seaside;

c. breakfast for a five-year-old on a cold winter's day;

d. a snack tea for a six-year-old and his friends in the middle of the summer holidays.

5. What advice would you offer to the parents of a young child who:

a. is insolent;

b. sucks his thumb;

c. behaves aggressively towards other children?

6. List some rules to remember when cleaning teeth. What is the difference between milk teeth and permanent teeth? Design a poster that will encourage young children to care for their teeth.

7. Make a simple musical instrument using kitchen "junk" and discarded household utensils. What musical activities would you expect to find in an infant school?

8. Arrange a class display of toys and games which are suitable for the young schoolchild. List some points to remember when buying toys for this age range.

9. Write a short paragraph on each of the following:

a. the value of play for the young schoolchild;

b. choosing footwear for a child;

c. bullying;

d. how a father can help with the responsibilities of bringing up young children.

10. Copy out this crossword and complete it.

Clues across

1. This is used to remove plaque from teeth.
2. A wart-like infection on the foot.
3. The compulsory school starting age.

Clues down

1. This helps to prevent decay in teeth.
4. A percussion instrument used in the infant school.
5. A method of teaching reading.

The health of the child

A healthy child is lively and cheerful. If a child becomes pale, listless and will not eat his meals, these are signs that all is not well. Here are some other signs.

1 A high temperature.   The normal body temperature is around 37°C. If a child's temperature rises to above 39°C, it is wise to consult a doctor. A very high temperature is dangerous and can lead to fever convulsions. A lower than usual temperature is also a sign of illness. To take a child's temperature:

   a use a clinical thermometer;
   b wipe under the armpit with a dry cloth and then place the bulb of the thermometer under the armpit and hold the child's arm against the side of his body;
   c after a minute, read the level of the mercury;
   d shake the thermometer so that the mercury recedes past the constriction or below 36·1°C;
   e wipe the thermometer with antiseptic fluid.

The temperature of a young baby can be taken by placing the thermometer in the rectum (back passage) but this method requires a special small bulb thermometer and should only be done by a doctor or trained nurse. The oral method (by mouth) is only suitable for older children who are not likely to bite on the thermometer and swallow the mercury.

If a child has a temperature:

   a put him to bed;
   b keep him cool by covering him with ***light*** bed-clothes, and sponging him down regularly with tepid or cool water;
   c give him plenty to drink;
   d try to bring the temperature down by giving para-cetamol or soluble aspirin; (***Do check on the dosage requirements suitable for the age of the child.***)
   e if the temperature is not down within 24 hours, consult a doctor.

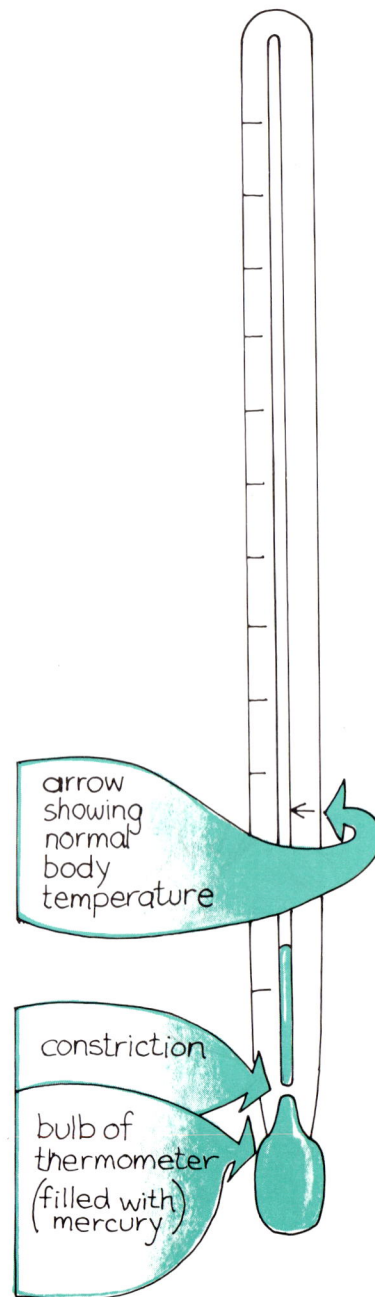

arrow showing normal body temperature

constriction

bulb of thermometer (filled with mercury)

2 Diarrhoea.　If a baby has diarrhoea for a few hours, he may become dehydrated. To combat this, always give plenty of boiled water or diluted milk to drink. In an older child, diarrhoea can be accompanied by abdominal pains. If the diarrhoea appears severe or the child looks ill, always consult a doctor.

3 Vomiting.　If a child is seldom sick and suddenly starts to vomit, this is a warning sign. Avoid all greasy foods and give him plenty of sweet liquids, e.g. fruit juices. If the vomiting persists, and is accompanied by diarrhoea or abdominal pains, send for the doctor.

4 Earache.　Earache can be a mild side effect of a cold, and this type of earache will disappear when the cold gets better. If a child suffers from persistent earache, has difficulty in hearing or has a discharge from the ear, consult a doctor immediately.

5 Coughing.　This may be a side effect of a cold and can be relieved with a patent cough medicine, or honey and lemon juice in hot water. If a child is wheezing or has a "croupy" cough, and shows difficulty in breathing, send for the doctor.

6 Difficulty in urinating.　If a baby does not have a wet nappy after six or eight hours, check with the doctor. If an older child has difficulty in urinating or has pain when passing water, an infection may be present. Always consult a doctor.

Infectious diseases of childhood

Many childhood ailments are infectious. This means that they can be passed on from one person to another by the spread of viruses and bacteria. Viruses and bacteria can be transmitted by:

direct contact with infected people

breathing infected air into the lungs

eating infected food

drinking infected water

germs penetrating broken areas of the skin

The period from the moment a person becomes infected to the time when the symptoms of a disease become apparent is called the ***incubation*** period. A person is most infectious and capable of spreading a disease just ***before*** and ***at the point when*** the first signs of the illness appear. Formerly, during the active period of an illness, an infected child was kept in ***quarantine***, i.e. isolated from other people, until the infection had passed. Nowadays, quarantine is rarely observed because:

a it is not successful in preventing the spread of an infection;

b it is considered safer for a child to catch an infectious disease and develop an immunity, than to risk becoming infected when an adult since many diseases are more serious for adults than for children.

A person can become immune or resistant to a particular disease by:

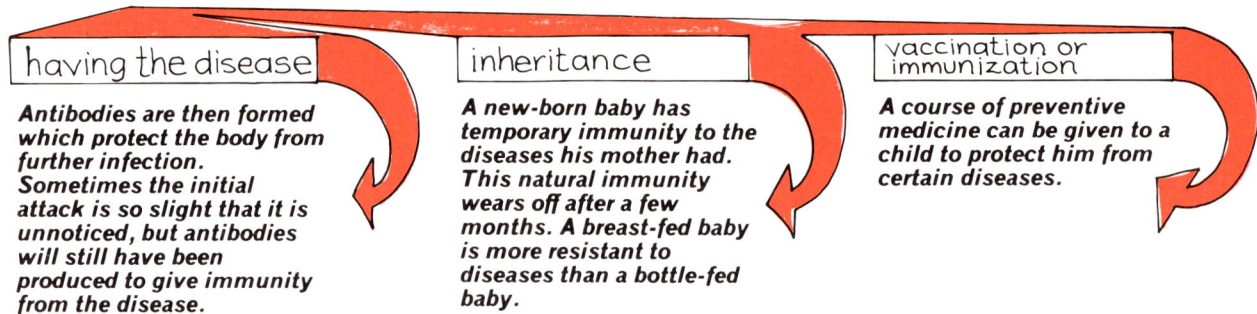

having the disease	inheritance	vaccination or immunization
Antibodies are then formed which protect the body from further infection. Sometimes the initial attack is so slight that it is unnoticed, but antibodies will still have been produced to give immunity from the disease.	**A new-born baby has temporary immunity to the diseases his mother had. This natural immunity wears off after a few months. A breast-fed baby is more resistant to diseases than a bottle-fed baby.**	**A course of preventive medicine can be given to a child to protect him from certain diseases.**

A table showing the common infectious diseases of childhood, and how they should be treated is on pages 134–5.

How to care for a sick child

Unless a child has a high temperature and is feeling very ill, there is no need to keep him in bed. A very sick child will not need persuading. He will be only too anxious to curl up in bed and remain quiet. When a child is staying in bed during the day, he should be covered with light bedclothes, and the bedroom should be well ventilated. If a child has a temperature, he should be dressed in cool, absorbent pyjamas, and changed frequently. A sweating child should be sponged down regularly to keep him cool and comfortable.

Paracetamol or soluble aspirin can be given to relieve head-aches and fever, but doses should be checked carefully.

Here are some more points to remember.

1 Any prescribed medicine must be taken. If this proves difficult:

a tablets can be crushed and mixed with jam or honey;

b soluble tablets can be dissolved in water;

c strongly flavoured medicines can be diluted by stirring them into pleasant drinks;

d sweets or chocolates can be offered as a reward.

Antibiotic medicine must be given at regular intervals, and the course of treatment should be completed, even when a child appears to be better.

2 A sick child should not be forced to eat. His appetite will return when he has recovered from the illness. Fluids are necessary though, and should be offered frequently. Fruit juices which are rich in vitamin C are beneficial, and milk can be offered in as many ways as possible, e.g. malted milk drinks, milk shakes, drinking chocolate. When a child is recovering from an illness he should be encouraged to eat by being offered small helpings of attractive looking dishes.

3 If a sick child does not want to stay in bed he can be dressed sensibly and brought into the lounge. He can lie on a couch if he still feels listless and tired. Being with an adult or his brothers and sisters will help to occupy him and keep him from feeling miserable. A shared activity, such as a jigsaw or card game, can help to alleviate boredom.

When a sick child starts to feel better, individual activity can be encouraged, e.g. Plasticene work, painting and crayoning, making a scrapbook with scissors, paste and old magazines, and playing with a constructional toy. Furniture can always be protected with plastic sheets or tablecloths, and untidiness should be overlooked for once. A sick child will enjoy having a story read to him, and when he feels better, a new book or toy will be a welcome treat. Suitable television programmes can be watched.

4 As soon as he is well enough, he should be allowed outside to get some fresh air and exercise. Friends can be encouraged round to play, but their parents should be informed if a child is still infectious.

Disease	Incubation Period	Symptoms of illness	Treatment
Measles	*8 to 12 days*	Starts with symptoms of a bad cold. A high temperature develops. White spots appear inside the mouth. A rash of pink/red spots starts behind the ears and spreads to the body and limbs. Spots turn into raised blotchy patches.	Notify the doctor. Keep the child in bed until his temperature drops. Usually paracetamol or soluble aspirin is all the medicine that is required. Give a light diet with plenty of liquids. A darkened room is advisable. If a child complains about eyes, ears or breathing, send for the doctor.
Whooping cough	*6 to 18 days*	Starts as a severe cold in the head, with a high temperature. A persistent cough develops and the child makes a "whoop" when breathing in between coughing spasms. This characteristic noise is not present in very young children.	Send for the doctor who may prescribe antibiotics. Give a light diet with plenty of liquids, only **after** a coughing spasm. Watch for signs of ear or lung infection. (This illness can be prevented by immunization.)
Mumps	*17 to 21 days*	Starts with pain and stiffness in the neck and jaw. Swelling appears on one or both sides of the jaw. There may be a loss of appetite, a headache and a temperature. Boys may feel tender around the scrotum. Girls may have abdominal pain.	Keep the child in bed until his temperature drops. Paracetamol or soluble aspirin can be given. Give a light diet with soft solids that do not need chewing, and plenty to drink. A warm scarf or shawl wrapped around the neck and face may help.

Disease	Incubation Period	Symptoms of illness	Treatment
Chickenpox	*14 to 21 days*	There may be a slight fever and headache at the onset of the illness. Small, clear blisters appear in crops. They usually spread to all parts of the body. Blisters dry up to form scabs or itchy crusts. Blisters may form in the mouth and throat causing pain and difficulty when swallowing.	Only keep the child in bed if he feels poorly. Relieve itching by covering scabs with calamine lotion. Try to stop the child from scratching the scabs. This can cause scarring. Cut nails short and, if necessary, get the child to wear cotton gloves.
German measles (*Rubella*)	*14 to 21 days*	There may be a slight fever and a tenderness in the joints with enlarged glands at the back of the neck. Usually a mild disease. A rash of small, flat, pink spots covers the body for 1 to 3 days.	Keep the child away from pregnant women. This disease can damage a young foetus. (If a girl has not been in contact with German measles and thus developed immunity to the disease, she can be vaccinated when 11 to 13 years of age.)
Scarlet Fever	*2 to 5 days*	This can start abruptly with a sore throat, temperature, loss of appetite and vomiting. Tonsils are very red and swollen. The tongue has a strawberry-like appearance. A fine, red rash appears on the body. The face becomes flushed. As the rash fades, the skin starts to peel.	Keep the child in bed and send for the doctor. Antibiotics may be prescribed. Give plenty of fluids. A mouthwash or gargle may be soothing.

Going into hospital

When a young child has to go into hospital it can be a bewildering and frightening event. If he also finds himself separated from his parents and family, he will feel insecure, lonely and upset. This separation can lead to long-lasting emotional problems. Most hospitals now provide facilities for a parent to stay in hospital with a child. When this is not possible, because of the needs of other young children in a family, visiting should be as frequent and as long as possible.

When there is advance warning of a hospital admission, a child should be prepared thoroughly for the event.

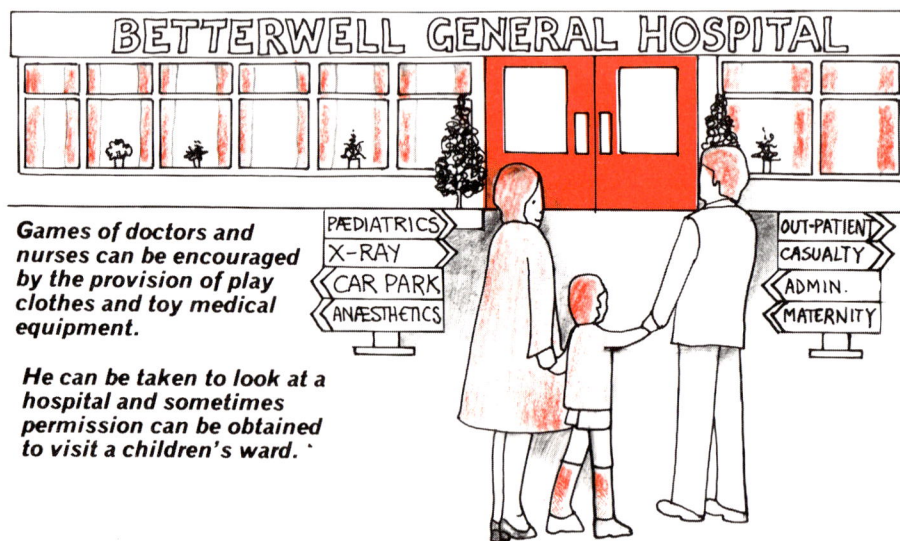

Games of doctors and nurses can be encouraged by the provision of play clothes and toy medical equipment.

He can be taken to look at a hospital and sometimes permission can be obtained to visit a children's ward. '

Library books can be read that tell stories about children in hospital. (A list of suitable books can be obtained from: The National Association for the Welfare of Children in Hospital, Exton House, 7 Exton Street, London SE1 8VE.)

A child should be told what is likely to happen to him in hospital. He should be told honestly that treatment may hurt and be unpleasant but that the doctors and nurses will help him to get better.

On the hospital admission of a child, a parent should:
a stay with him, if at all possible, or visit frequently;
b be calm and reassuring;
c check that the child's favourite toy or "comforter" is taken into hospital with him.

A parent should never promise to visit a child and then not do so. This could cause a child to feel abandoned. A goodbye kiss and cuddle, followed by an assurance that the next visit will be at "such and such a time" is much better than a sudden disappearance when a child's attention has been diverted.

Preventive medicine

A child can be protected from some diseases by being immunized or vaccinated. Certain illnesses are caused when **toxins** (poisons) enter the body. If a person has not built up antibodies to fight off the infection, his body is not able to resist the toxins, and a severe illness results. Immunization consists of injecting the person with weakened or altered forms of the toxin. This produces a very mild form of the disease, but ensures that antibodies are developed to protect against further infection. Listed below are diseases which can be prevented by immunization.

Diphtheria.   This used to be a very serious illness which sometimes proved fatal. It produced an infection of the throat and also affected the heart. Immunization in the early 1940s brought the disease under control, and cases of diphtheria are now not very common.

Tetanus.   This disease, sometimes called lock-jaw, can affect children and adults. When dirt and germs enter an open wound, toxins can cause painful muscle spasms, particularly in the neck.

Tetanus can prove fatal. A course of 3 injections during early childhood, followed by regular 4-yearly booster jabs, gives complete protection from this disease. It is possible to give a tetanus injection at the time of an injury, but better protection is afforded by immunization in childhood.

Whooping cough. Whooping cough is rarely serious in older children but in young children it can prove fatal or lead to severe complications of the respiratory system. Immunization in early childhood gives protection against the disease.

There is some evidence to suggest that there is a link between the whooping cough vaccine and rare cases of brain damage. (One child in every 300,000 children who receive the whooping cough vaccine may become permanently damaged.) Parents have to decide whether to refuse this vaccine and run the very slight risk of their child contracting whooping cough ***and*** suffering permanent damage from it, or accept the vaccine knowing that there is a remote possibility of brain damage.

Measles. Protection against measles can be given by a single injection of live vaccine sometime during a child's second year.

Polio(myelitis). This disease is highly infectious. It can cause meningitis and severe permanent paralysis. A dead (Salk) vaccine, which is injected, or a live (Sabin) vaccine, which is given orally, offers protection against the disease.

German measles *(Rubella).* If a pregnant woman becomes infected with German measles during the first three months of pregnancy, the foetus may become severely damaged. For this reason it is advisable for any girl in her teens, who has not built up antibodies against this disease, to have a single injection of the live vaccine. This is sensible preventive medicine.

Tuberculosis *(T.B.).* Immunization against tuberculosis is available to children between 10 and 13 years of age. A special test is performed which consists of injecting tuberculin into the skin. If the reaction is tuberculin-positive, then there is already immunity to the disease, and no further treatment is necessary. If the reaction is tuberculin-negative, B.C.G. vaccine can be used to give protection against it.

Smallpox. Vaccination against this is now only given when needed for foreign travel regulations, or in the event of an epidemic. The vaccine is placed on the upper arm and gently pricked into the skin.

Immunization timetables can vary slightly from region to region. This schedule of injections is often used.

Age	Immunization
4 to 6 months	1st dose of diphtheria/tetanus/whooping cough vaccine 1st dose of polio vaccine
6 to 8 months	2nd dose of diphtheria/tetanus/whooping cough vaccine 2nd dose of polio vaccine
12 to 14 months	3rd dose of diphtheria/tetanus/whooping cough vaccine 3rd dose of polio vaccine
15 to 24 months	Measles vaccine
5 years or on starting school	Booster dose of diphtheria/tetanus vaccine Booster dose of polio vaccine
10 to 13 years	Rubella vaccine B.C.G. vaccine (if tuberculin test is negative)
On leaving school	Booster dose of tetanus vaccine Booster dose of polio vaccine

The diphtheria, tetanus and whooping cough vaccines are usually combined into one "triple" vaccine. If a parent does not want a child to be given the whooping cough vaccine, he can still be immunized against diphtheria and tetanus.

Here are some points to remember about immunization.

1 If a child is unwell, immunization should be delayed.

2 Inform the doctor of any medicines or course of treatment a child may be taking at the time of the immunization.

3 Always notify the doctor if previous immunizations resulted in unusual side effects.

4 If a child suffers from eczema (a skin disease), he should not have the smallpox vaccine.

5 If a member of the family has a history of convulsions, epilepsy or a respiratory disease, the doctor should be told.

6 If there are unpleasant reactions in the 24 hours following immunization, the doctor should be notified. Look out for these signs:

7 Do keep a record of the date and type of each immunization. This information may be required in the future.

The Child Health Centre

A local Child Health Clinic or Centre is the place where parents can go regularly to:

have their baby weighed

socialize with other parents and their babies

discuss problems with the Health Visitor, who is a specially trained nurse

have their baby immunized

obtain supplies of vitamins and baby foods

see the doctor for regular medical check-ups, so that their baby's progress can be monitored

The Health Visitor makes a home visit to each mother and newly born baby in her area. Repeat visits are made where necessary. The Health Visitor is available at the clinic to offer advice, answer questions and generally look after the welfare of the children on her register. As a child grows up, arrangements will be made for routine examinations of his heart, lungs, hearing and vision. His mental and physical development will be monitored. If a child has a particular problem, e.g. a speech impediment or difficulty in walking, advice can be given and specialist help sought.

The School Health Service

On entry to school, each child is given a thorough medical check-up. Special tests are made to detect any hearing or sight problems, and these are referred for specialist treatment. A child will have at least three medical check-ups whilst at school.

A dentist will make regular checks for dental decay. Any treatment recommended can be had at the school dental clinic or from a child's own dentist.

The Health Visitor makes periodical checks for nits (the eggs of the head louse), and will also look at nails and feet.

If a child is having behavioural problems, he can be referred to an educational psychologist, a Child Guidance Clinic or an Education Welfare Officer.

Preventing accidents

Each year many children are injured or die as a result of accidents in the home and the environment. The majority of these accidents can be prevented. Let us consider the different kinds of hazards and how it is possible to guard against them.

Injuries or death can result from:

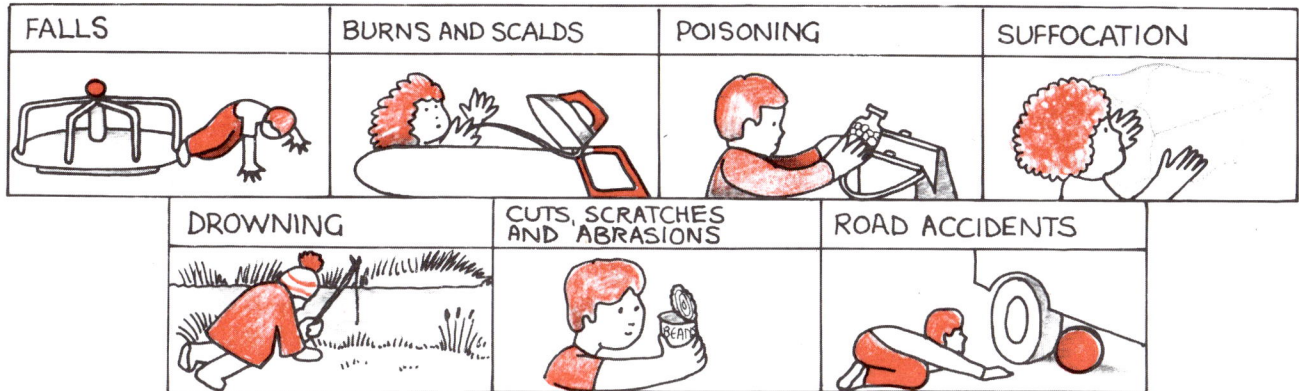

FALLS	BURNS AND SCALDS	POISONING	SUFFOCATION

DROWNING	CUTS, SCRATCHES AND ABRASIONS	ROAD ACCIDENTS

How to guard against falls

1 Always see that staircases, halls and landings are well lit.

2 Do not leave unexpected objects on the floor where they can be tripped over. Encourage a child to put his toys away after use.

3 Do not polish under loose mats.

4 See that the flexes from electrical appliances do not trail along the floor.

5 Check that worn floor coverings and mats are not in a dangerous condition.

6 Wipe up spilt liquids and greases as soon as they occur.

7 Check that a baby is securely fastened in his high chair, pushchair, pram or "baby bouncer".

8 Use safety gates to protect a toddler from falling down staircases, and from running out of the garden. Teach a young child how to climb staircases correctly.

9 Use a bath mat in the baby's bath. This will prevent slips.

10 Keep tables, chairs and stools away from windows, so that a child cannot climb on to window sills.

11 Fasten windows securely when leaving a room, especially windows that are at a low level.

12 Fix vertical bars to nursery and playroom windows. These should be removable in case of fire.

13 Heavy items of furniture should be secure and stable so that they cannot topple over when knocked or pulled.

14 Do not leave a tiny baby unattended on any high surface, e.g. bed, table top, couch. He may roll off on to the floor.

15 Do not let a small child play in public playgrounds unless you can watch him **all the time**. Do not let him play or run near any swings.

How to guard against burns and scalds

1 Always see that open fires, gas and electric fires are properly guarded.

2 Do not let a young child play near a washing machine or cooker that is being used.

3 The handles of saucepans should be turned to the back or sides of a cooker. A cooker guard, which is fixed around the hob of a cooker, makes it much harder for a child to tip saucepans over.

4 Run cold water into a bath, before turning on the hot tap.

5 Check that a child cannot reach teapots, cups of tea and any hot dishes on a table.

6 Do not let tablecloths trail.

7 Do not put a child's toys or any fancy ornaments on the mantlepiece above an unguarded fire.

8 Always keep matches, lighter fuels and inflammable solutions away from a young child.

9 Do not dry or air clothes near an unguarded fire.

10 Do not use an oil heater in a position where it might be knocked over. **Never** move an oil heater when it is lit. Do not leave a young child alone in a room with a lighted oil heater.

11 Buy non-inflammable or flame resistant clothing, whenever possible. This is especially important for a child's nightwear.

12 Always be wary of fireworks. Store them safely. Use them sensibly. Do not let a young child play with them.

13 Try to teach a child which household items are inflammable, e.g. aerosol canisters, cleaning fluids.

14 Keep the flexes of electrical appliances out of the reach of a child. Irons, kettles and heated hair rollers are particularly dangerous.

15 Do not carry a cup of tea, a teapot or a tea tray over a child's head.

16 If a night-light is being left in a child's bedroom, it should be placed well out of the way.

How to guard against poisoning

1 Check that all gas appliances are serviced regularly. Do not let a child play with gas taps or gas meters.

2 If the gas supply is cut, turn off all gas taps immediately. When the gas supply comes on, check that all pilot lights are lit.

3 Always ensure that there is adequate ventilation in rooms that have a gas appliance. This is especially important if water is heated by a gas geyser in a bathroom.

4 Keep all medicines in a special cabinet. This should have a childproof safety catch or be locked, if there is a young child in the house.

5 Never store cleaning fluids or chemicals in empty soft drink bottles. Always keep bleach and disinfectants away from a child.
6 Teach a child not to eat things that he may find in the garden, e.g. berries, laburnum seeds, fungi.
7 Keep weedkillers and all garden chemicals in a locked cupboard in the garage or garden shed.
8 Keep all medicines in the bottles in which they were prescribed. Check that all medicines are labelled clearly. When buying patent medicines, look for childproof bottles.

How to guard against suffocation (asphyxia)
1 Do not let a young baby sleep on a pillow.
2 Never let a child play with a plastic bag.
3 Do not leave a baby to feed himself, by propping a bottle in his mouth.
4 Always check that a baby has "brought up wind" before putting him down to sleep.
5 A baby or young child should not sleep in the same bed as his parents, because of the danger that they might accidentally lie on top of him.
6 Do not leave a plastic-backed bib around a baby's neck after a feed.
7 Use a safety net to prevent family pets from sleeping on prams, pushchairs and cots.
8 See that old, airtight appliances, e.g. refrigerators, cookers and freezers, are removed by the local authority. If this cannot be done immediately, take off doors that have catches or locks.
9 Do not let a toddler play with tiny objects which could be pushed up the nose or inhaled accidentally, e.g. small beads, peanuts, dried peas and pasta shapes.
10 Teach a young child the dangers involved in putting things around his neck. Avoid using roller towels.
11 Check that the folding mechanism on a pram and pushchair is childproof.

How to guard against drowning
1 Garden ponds should be covered or fenced around, if there is a young child about.

TOXIC

this is dangerous

2 Paddling pools should be emptied immediately after use.
3 A young child should be taught the dangers of rivers, ponds, lakes, reservoirs, the sea, wells, mine shafts and gravel pits.
4 Never leave a child alone in the bath.
5 Always supervise any water play activities.
6 Cover water butts and storage barrels.
7 Never leave a filled washing machine unattended.
8 Encourage all members of the family to learn to swim.
9 Encourage all members of the family to learn to life-save, and make sure they know how to give artificial respiration in an emergency.

How to guard against cuts, scratches and abrasions

1 Do not leave sharp utensils where a young child may be able to reach them. Be careful with scissors, old razor blades and jagged tins.
2 Wrap broken crockery and glass in newspaper, and put it in the dustbin.
3 Do not let a young child carry or play with breakable crockery.
4 Put pins and needles away safely.

How to guard against accidents on the road

1 House doors and garden gates should be kept closed so that a young child cannot run on to the road. Safety gates should be fitted, if necessary, to block all possible exits.
2 Never let a child play in an open street.
3 Do not let a young child run from the garden to retrieve a ball or talk to a friend. Explain the dangers involved with traffic.
4 Teach a child the Green Cross Code. If there is a local Tufty Club, take him along to learn road safety.
5 Teach a child the dangers involved in crossing a road between parked vehicles.
6 When parking a pram, always check that the brake is on securely. When crossing a road, always make sure that the road is clear before pushing the pram over the kerb.
7 Do not let a young child run to an ice-cream van by himself. Explain the dangers involved.

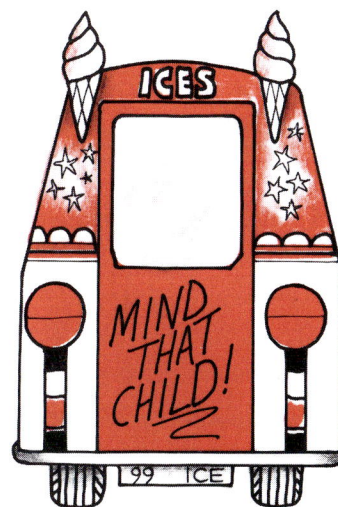

8 If a carrycot is put on the back seat of a car, it should be strapped firmly in position. A special safety seat should be used for a toddler, and an older child should wear a seat belt.

9 Check that car doors are closed correctly and that the childproof safety locks are in position.

10 If driving a car, be particularly careful if you notice children playing at the side of the road. Slow down when you approach a school building, and do not park directly outside the school gates.

11 Always double check using your driving mirror before reversing into a parking space. There could be a small child stepping off the pavement.

12 If you see a ball rolling into the road ahead of you, slow down. There may be a child running after the ball.

Simple first aid

Every home should have a special first aid kit which is equipped with all the necessary items for dealing with minor accidents. First aid supplies should be kept in a lidded container, which is stored beyond the reach of a small child. It is not a good idea to lock the first aid kit. In an emergency, precious minutes may be lost in searching for the key.

A home first aid kit should contain:

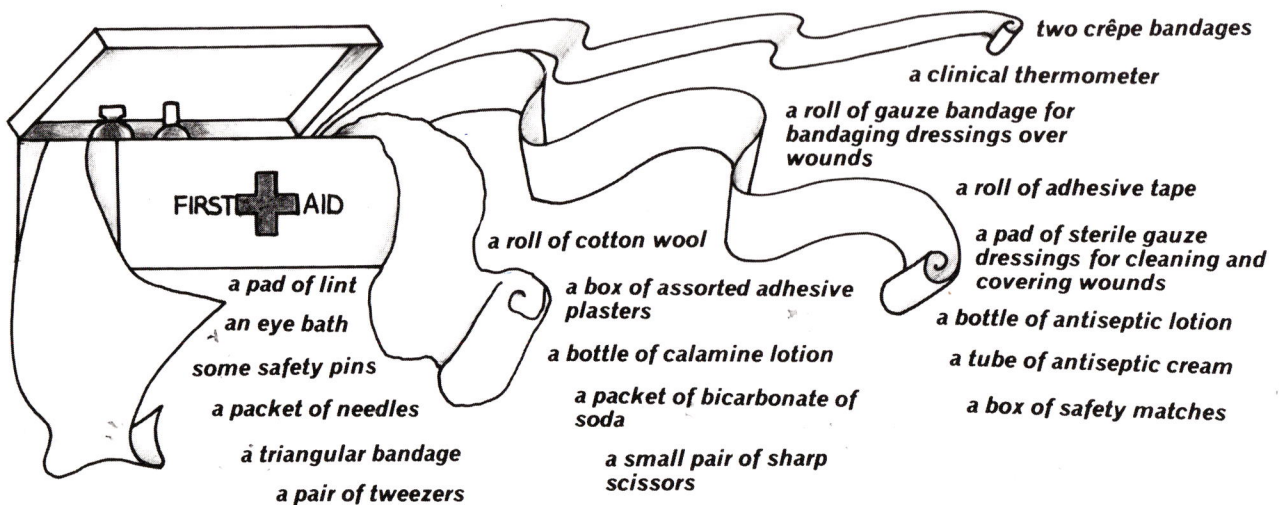

FIRST AID

two crêpe bandages

a clinical thermometer

a roll of gauze bandage for bandaging dressings over wounds

a roll of adhesive tape

a pad of sterile gauze dressings for cleaning and covering wounds

a roll of cotton wool

a box of assorted adhesive plasters

a bottle of antiseptic lotion

a tube of antiseptic cream

a box of safety matches

a pad of lint

an eye bath

some safety pins

a packet of needles

a bottle of calamine lotion

a packet of bicarbonate of soda

a triangular bandage

a pair of tweezers

a small pair of sharp scissors

Medicines, such as paracetamol, soluble aspirin, cough linctus, prescribed medicaments etc. should be kept in a separate childproof medicine cabinet.

Here are some points to remember when treating a child for a minor accident.

1 A minor cut, scratch or abrasion should be cleaned thoroughly with sterile gauze and running cold water. Antiseptic lotion or cream can be applied to the wound, which should then be covered with an adhesive plaster, a piece of sterile gauze held in place by a bandage, or a piece of sterile gauze held in place with adhesive tape.

2 If a child has swallowed a poisonous substance, take him immediately to the casualty department of a hospital, or to the doctor. Do **not** try to make him vomit. This can be very dangerous. If it is obvious which poison a child has swallowed, take the bottle or container along with you. This will help the doctor to identify the treatment required.

3 When a child has a head injury, observe him closely for the next 24 hours. If there are any signs of sudden drowsiness, fainting or vomiting, the child should be taken immediately to the casualty department, or to see the doctor. After any head injury, a child may suffer from shock. Loosen any tight clothing and keep him warm.

4 A minor burn or scald should be immersed in cold water immediately. After about 10 minutes, the area should be covered with a dry sterile dressing. A clean handkerchief can be used in an emergency. Do **not** try to remove any clothing from a bad burn. Take the child to the casualty department or doctor, as quickly as possible.

5 If a child is choking over swallowed food or an inhaled object, encourage him to cough. If this does not dislodge the object, hold his head downwards and pat him vigorously between the shoulder blades. Artificial respiration can be used if a child's breathing stops. If the swallowed object is not expelled from the mouth, it is wise to see a doctor to check that the object has not entered the lungs.

6 Do not try to remove a foreign object from the ear. Take the child to the doctor. If an object is lodged in the nose, encourage the child to blow his nose vigorously. If this is unsuccessful, see the doctor.

7 When treating a nosebleed, encourage the child to breathe through his mouth. Sit the child with his head forward over a bowl, and press or pinch the nostrils together for at least 5 minutes. If this fails to stop the bleeding, try plugging each nostril with sterile gauze preferably or cotton wool if there is no gauze available, but leave an end hanging loosely so that the plug can be removed.

8 If a child is stung by a bee or wasp, try to remove the sting by lifting it out with a sterile needle or pair of tweezers. Run cold water on to the affected area and cover with an ice cube. This will numb the pain and slow down the absorption of the venom. Apply antiseptic lotion. If a child has any unusual symptoms after being stung, do see a doctor.

9 If a child is suffering from sunburn, apply calamine lotion to the affected parts of the skin. Cover the sunburned areas with lightweight clothing.

10 A sprained or strained muscle should be bathed in iced cold water to reduce the swelling, and then wrapped in a firm bandage. After a period of rest the swelling should disappear.

11 If a child suffers from epileptic fits, try to prevent injury by removing any obstruction as the child falls. If possible, put a knotted handkerchief or hard, smooth object between the teeth, to prevent the child from biting his tongue. After an attack, place the child in the recovery position (see diagram below), and stay with him until he has regained consciousness.

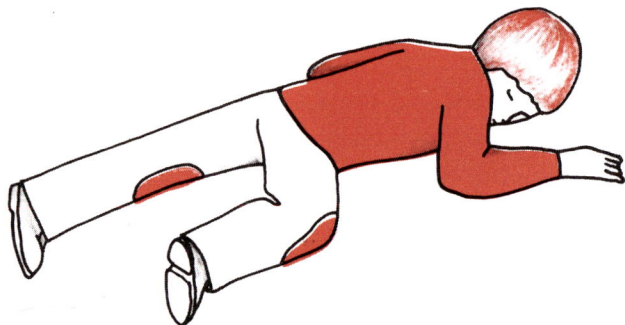

12 To apply artificial respiration by mouth to mouth resuscitation:

    a loosen any tight clothing and clear the mouth of any obstruction;
    b push the head backwards to extend the neck;
    c close the nostrils by pinching them tightly together;
    d open the mouth and pull the jaw forward;
    e blow into the mouth;
    f let the chest deflate. Continue rythmically blowing into the mouth once every 4 or 5 seconds until the doctor arrives.

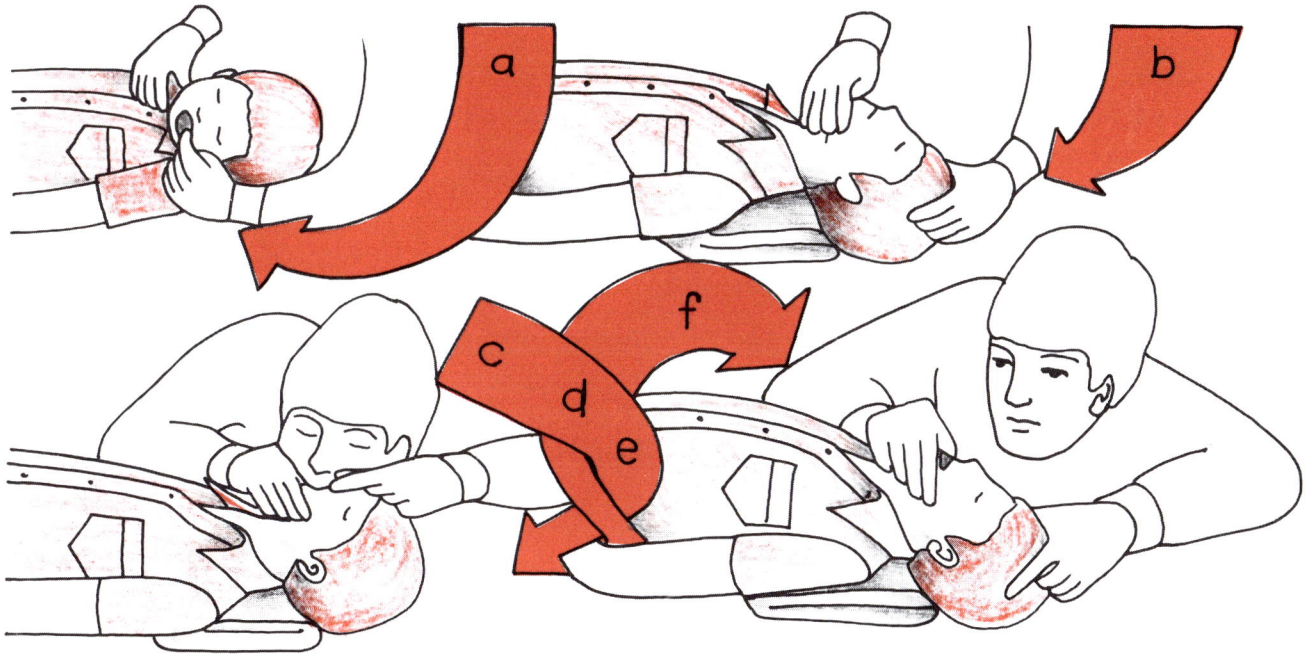

Think and Do

1. Design a poster that will explain the advantages of child immunization.

2. What advice would you give to a young parent whose child is in bed with a feverish headache and sore throat?

3. List *four* ways in which you could prevent accidents to children in each of the following places:
a. the home;
b. the garden;
c. the street.
4. List *ten* items you would expect to find in a home first aid kit. How would you treat each of the following:
a. a scald;
b. a grazed knee;
c. an insect sting;
d. shock following a bad fall;
e. sunburn;
f. a sprained ankle?
5. Copy the following diagram into your notebook. In the boxes, write a description of the symptoms of each illness and what treatment should be given.

CHILDHOOD AILMENTS

Measles	Whooping cough	Mumps	Chicken pox	German measles	Scarlet fever

6. What is meant by each of the following:
a. the incubation period of an infectious illness;
b. an oral vaccine;
c. a tuberculin-negative reaction to a skin test;
d. immunity to a disease?
7. Write a paragraph on each of the following:
a. taking a child's temperature;
b. preparing a child for hospital admission;
c. nursing a sick child;
d. giving mouth to mouth resuscitation.
8. Visit your school and local libraries and find out all you can about Edward Jenner's work on preventive medicine.

9. Name *two* benefits provided by the School Health Service. What is the role of the Health Visitor?

10. Copy out this crossword and complete it.

Clues across

1. This medicine will help to bring down a high temperature.
2. Suffocation.
3. A poison.
4. A virus used in vaccination.

Clues down

5. A child who suffers from eczema should not be vaccinated against this disease.
6. It can cause a baby to become dehydrated.
7. The eggs of the head louse.
8. German measles.

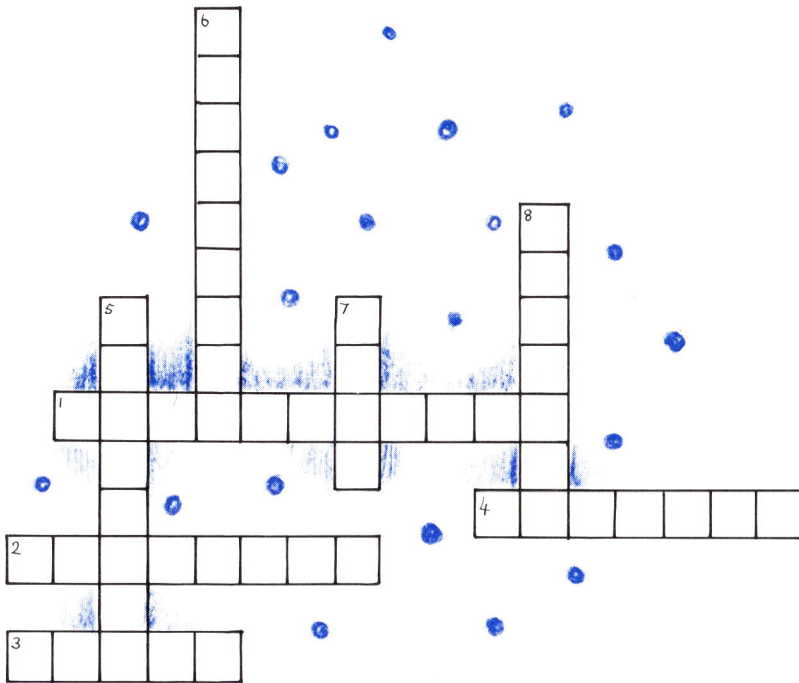

Adoption and fostering

Adoption

Adoption is a legal process during which all the parental rights, duties and obligations of a child's parents are transferred to his adoptive parents. The adoptive parents assume complete responsibility for the future welfare, education and upbringing of the child, and the adopted child receives the legal status of a "child born in wedlock".

The process of adoption concerns three groups of people: *1* the mother, or natural parents of a child (if married); *2* the child; *3* the prospective adopters.

The mother, or natural parents of the child (if married)

The majority of children for adoption are the illegitimate children of unmarried mothers. An unmarried mother is faced with financial, emotional and social problems if she wants to keep her baby, and she may decide that her child will stand a better chance in life, if he has two parents and a secure and stable family background. The decision whether to keep her baby or have him adopted, must be made by the mother but these people will give help and advice.

1 Social workers in the children's department of the local authority where the mother lives
2 The family doctor
3 The local Health Visitor
4 A registered adoption society
5 A minister of religion, who may also be able to put the mother in contact with a church-related voluntary organization for the Unmarried Mother and Her Child
6 The National Council for the Unmarried Mother and Her Child *or* the Scottish Council for the Unmarried Mother and Her Child
7 The National Council for One-Parent Families
8 Hospital-based social workers
9 The Samaritans

A married woman who conceives by a man who is not her husband, may decide to have the baby adopted, so that her existing marriage can be saved.

Adoption may also be considered by a married couple who, because of social, medical or emotional reasons, cannot keep their legitimate child. These cases are very rare. A married couple would be more likely to have their child fostered, than sever the natural family ties altogether by placing him for adoption.

When the parents of a young child die, a relative or guardian may decide to legally adopt the child. If this is not possible, other prospective adopters may be sought.

The mother, parents or legal guardian of a child must agree to the adoption, and the formal document of consent should be witnessed by a Justice of the Peace, a County Court Officer or a Justice's Clerk (in Scotland, a Sheriff or a Justice of the Peace). A mother's formal consent is not valid until the child is six weeks old.

An adoption does not become final until an adoption order is granted by:

the High Court	or	the County Court	or	the Juvenile Court

the Court of Session	or	the Sheriff Court	→ in Scotland

It is possible for the mother, parent or legal guardian to withdraw their consent to the adoption at any stage up to the signing of the final adoption order. If, however, they change their mind after the consent form has been signed and the application to adopt has been submitted to the court, the child cannot be removed from the prospective adopters unless the court gives its permission. The court may rule that it is in the child's best interests to stay with the prospective adopters, and will therefore proceed to sign the adoption order.

The child

Adoption aims at finding a good home for a child, rather than providing prospective adopters with a suitable child. The emphasis is on the welfare of the child, and the social worker who is experienced in adoption law and procedure will make many visits to prospective adopters before and after the placement of the child to check on the suitability of the adopters and the welfare of the child placed with them.

A child can be placed with prospective adopters when he is only a few days old, but legally he cannot be considered for adoption until he is six weeks old. (The mother's formal consent is not valid until then.)

Here are some of the advantages and disadvantages of placing a new-born baby with prospective adopters.

Advantages	Disadvantages
1 The baby has a continuous loving and caring relationship with two parents.	1 The natural mother has to give a hurried decision. (This can be offset by experienced counselling from a social worker before the birth of the child.)
2 There is less chance that the baby will suffer neglect and rejection.	2 The baby cannot be breast-fed.
3 If the natural mother keeps the baby for a short period and then has to give him for adoption, she will have become emotionally involved, and the parting will be worse.	3 There is less time to monitor the baby's probable physical, mental and emotional development.
4 There is more chance of his personality becoming disturbed if he is cared for in a local authority nursery or community home.	
5 The prospective adopters will be able to accept a tiny baby more readily than an older child.	
6 Physical characteristics are inherited but many mannerisms are acquired through imitation. The younger the baby, the more he will be able to identify with his adoptive parents.	
7 The younger the baby, the more he will be influenced by the environment of his adoptive parents.	

A toddler or older child who is being adopted, should be introduced gradually to the prospective adopters. Frequent "getting to know each other" sessions will help to overcome the difficulties of the settling in period, when the child is actually placed for adoption on a permanent basis.

If a child is old enough to understand the implications of adoption, his wishes are considered by the court before the adoption order is finally granted.

The prospective adopters

There are three different ways that prospective adopters can find a child.

1 Through an adoption agency.   This can be one of a number of registered voluntary adoption societies, or it can be the Social Services Committee (the Social Work Committee in Scotland).

2 By dealing directly with the mother, parents or guardian.   A child can be placed directly with prospective adopters by his mother, parents, or legal guardian. If the placement proves to be detrimental to the child's welfare, the local authority can remove the child and take him into care.

3 Through a third party.   This can be any individual who agrees to place a child with prospective adopters e.g. a doctor, neighbour, friend or relative. He is required by law to notify the Director of Social Services 14 days before the proposed placing of the child. The local authority is entitled to visit the prospective adopters and may veto the placement if it is considered unsuitable.

Adopting through an agency has many advantages, and prospective adopters are often advised to use this means. An adoption agency has skilled social workers who are experienced in the legal aspects of adoption, and are qualified to advise and help all the parties concerned.

Each adoption agency has its own rules and regulations, but prospective adopters are usually expected to:

a have been happily married for a few years;
b be within the normal age range of natural parenthood (by law adopters must be at least twenty-one years old);

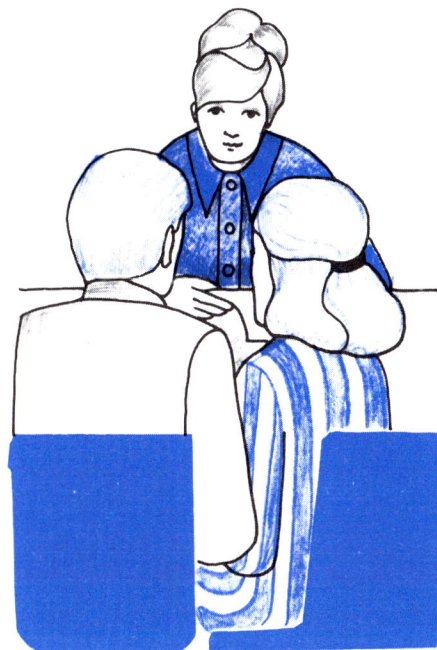

c be healthy (a medical examination may be required);

d have an adequately sized and furnished home;

e give details of their income, financial security and future prospects;

f supply the names and addresses of at least two referees;

g undergo a period of observation and home visits by a social worker, so that their motives and suitability as adopters can be ascertained.

Here are some useful addresses for prospective adopters.

1 The Association of British Adoption and Fostering Agencies, 4, Southampton Row, London WC1B 4AA

2 Parent to Parent Information on Adoption Services, 26, Belsize Grove, London NW3

Adoption certificates

A copy of each adoption order is sent to the Registrar General, and the adopted child's new name is entered on the Adopted Children's Register. A shortened form of the adoption order, leaving out details of the child's original parentage, is sent to the adopters. This shortened form of the adoption certificate resembles a short birth certificate.

Access to original birth records

The Children Act 1975 made it possible for an adopted person, who wished to trace his natural parentage, to see his original birth certificate. Previously this information could only be revealed with a court order. The Act stipulates that a person who was adopted before 1975 should attend an interview with a counsellor, before being given access to his birth records, but a person adopted after 1975 need not do so.

Telling a child that he is adopted

It is very important that an adopted child grows up knowing and understanding that he is adopted. If a person is not told about his adoption until he is in his teens, the knowledge can come as a shattering blow, and he may find it difficult to accept the situation. There are many ways in which parents can help a child to understand.

1 A child should be told that he is adopted at a very early age. When the word is used repeatedly, it becomes accepted. Even though a young child may not understand the implications, he will grow up linking the word "adopted" with feeling loved, happy and secure.

2 Parents may wish to emphasize that being adopted is something special. They can remind a child that he was chosen by them, and that this was a sign of how much they loved and wanted him.

3 A complete record of his early life should be kept, including as many photographs as possible. When the child grows older, this tangible evidence of his "belonging" to the family, will prove valuable.

4 There are many library books which give the facts about adoption in story form, and are suitable for reading to pre-school children. These books can be read as an introduction to talking about adoption, or as a means of reminding a child that he is adopted.

5 It is helpful to mark the anniversary of the date of an adoption. This could become a special family occasion.

6 Parents of an adopted child should be prepared to discuss the subject of adoption whenever a suitable opportunity arises. It is not sufficient to tell a child that he is adopted, and then to avoid any subsequent reference to the fact. A child may want to ask questions or just talk about the subject, but may feel uncomfortable about opening the conversation. It is important that questions about a child's natural parents are answered honestly and fairly, in simple language that a child can understand.

7 If an older child wants to trace his original parentage, his adoptive parents should accept the fact and try to be as helpful and understanding as possible. A leaflet which lists the rights of an adopted person to trace his natural parentage, can be obtained from the General Register Office (CA Section), Titchfield, Fareham, Hants.

Fostering

A child may have to be taken into care by the Social Services Department or by a voluntary organization, for any of the reasons given over the page.

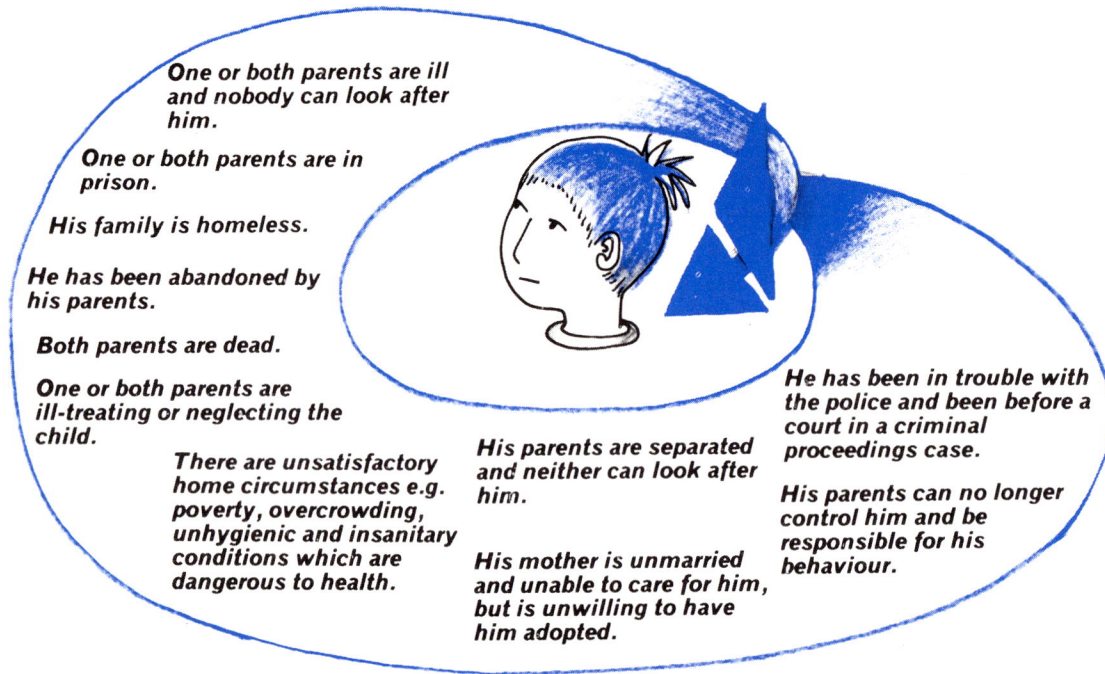

One or both parents are ill and nobody can look after him.

One or both parents are in prison.

His family is homeless.

He has been abandoned by his parents.

Both parents are dead.

One or both parents are ill-treating or neglecting the child.

There are unsatisfactory home circumstances e.g. poverty, overcrowding, unhygienic and insanitary conditions which are dangerous to health.

His parents are separated and neither can look after him.

His mother is unmarried and unable to care for him, but is unwilling to have him adopted.

He has been in trouble with the police and been before a court in a criminal proceedings case.

His parents can no longer control him and be responsible for his behaviour.

When the Social Services Department assumes responsibility for a child who is deprived of a normal home, they agree to provide accommodation and maintenance for the child. This can be for a period of weeks until the child is able to return home, or it can be for the whole of his childhood until he reaches the age of eighteen. During this time the local authority will supervise his care and general welfare. The Social Services Department aims to provide a happy, caring atmosphere for the child, until the time that the special problems and difficulties which brought him into care, have been resolved.

The local authority has to decide what kind of accommodation will suit the child best. Some children are happier in a large community home, where there are fewer emotional ties. Other children prefer to live as part of a small family unit. Sometimes arrangements can be made to board a child with a guardian, relative or friend, but if this is not possible he can be accommodated in:

   a a community children's home run either by the local authority or a voluntary organization;

   b a short stay foster home;

   c a long stay foster home.

A foster parent is one who agrees to look after somebody else's child until the child is able to return to his own home. A foster parent must return a foster child, if he is required to do so by the natural parents or the local authority.

Whilst a child is being fostered, he will be visited regularly by a social worker who will check that the child is happy and being looked after well. The social worker will also help and advise the foster parents, and try to keep the foster child in touch with his natural parents. This can be done by visits, letters or telephone calls. A good foster parent will encourage such links with the natural parents, even when there seems little chance of a child ever returning home. Some children stay permanently in their foster homes, and others are fostered and subsequently adopted.

When a child is in the care of the local authority his natural parents are required to make some contribution towards his maintenance, until the child reaches the age of sixteen. Foster parents receive financial assistance from the Social Services Department.

Think and Do

1. What advice would you give to an unmarried mother who is considering placing her child for adoption?

2. Explain the differences between adoption and fostering.

3. What are the usual requirements and qualifications of prospective adopters?

4. What is the role of the social worker? How can he be of help to:

a. foster parents;

b. prospective adopters?

5. Suggest ways in which a parent can help a child to understand and accept that he is adopted.

6. Name *two* kinds of family problem that may result in a child being taken into care by a local authority. Under the heading "Residential accommodation for children in care", write a brief description of each of the following:

a. community children's homes;

b. short stay foster homes;

c. long stay foster homes.

7. Find out where you would go or what you would do, to:

a. become a foster parent;

b. obtain information about the various adoption societies;

c. apply for an adoption order.

8. Copy out the following sentences. Say whether each one is *true* or *false*.

a. A person wishing to adopt a child must be at least twenty-one years old.

b. When a child is fostered he severs all connections with his natural family.

c. An adoption agency must be registered with the local authority.

d. An adoption does not become final until an adoption order has been granted.

e. A local authority will look after children in care until they reach the age of sixteen.

f. The Children Act 1975 made it possible for an adopted person to trace his original parentage.

9. Copy the following diagram into your notebook. Write a suitable sentence in each of the boxes.

DIFFERENT WAYS OF ADOPTING

Through an adoption agency	By dealing directly with the mother, parents or guardian	Through a third party

10. List some of the advantages and disadvantages of an early adoption.

The handicapped child and families with special problems

An education authority is responsible for the education of all the children in its area. This means that arrangements must be made for the special needs of:

a the physically handicapped child;

b the mentally handicapped child;

c the maladjusted child who is handicapped by his environment.

A handicapped child can be considered for special educational measures from the age of two, but parents cannot be compelled to accept special schooling for a child until he is five years old. The 1978 Warnock report on handicapped children, though, strongly recommends that special education should be begun before the age of five.

Some handicaps are not easy to identify in a very young child. Hearing, sight and speech problems may only become apparent when a child starts to talk, look at books and read. It is very important that a child receives the regular health checks and developmental tests that are available at local Child Health Centres, so that any specific disability can be detected early.

When it is suspected that a child may need special schooling because of a physical, mental or environmental handicap, he is referred to the local education authority for a medical examination. A child can be sent for a medical assessment by his:

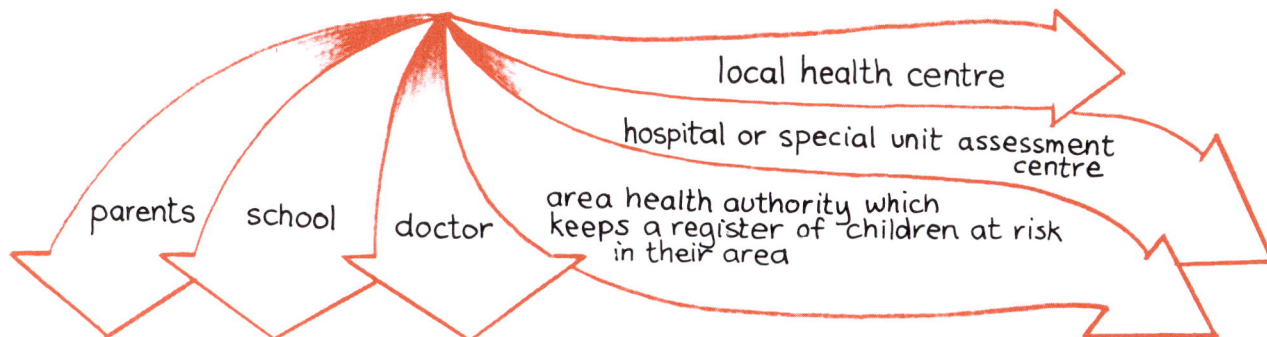

parents

school

doctor

area health authority which keeps a register of children at risk in their area

local health centre

hospital or special unit assessment centre

The results of the medical examination determine whether or not a child can be educated in an ordinary school. If special schooling is required, this can be provided in:

    a a special unit or class attached to an ordinary school;
    b a special school (day or boarding);
    c a hospital school;
    d the home.

Many ordinary schools, especially in cities, have special units or classes which cater for the handicapped child. A child in one of these units is able to benefit from specialized equipment and teaching methods, but is also able to join in many of the ordinary school activities. This integration into an ordinary school helps the handicapped child to feel less isolated, and encourages him to socialize and make friends with normal children of his own age. Separating the normal and the handicapped child prevents each from understanding the needs of the other.

If a local education authority cannot offer facilities for the special schooling needed, it can either offer the handicapped child a boarding place at a suitable special school, or it can provide board and lodging so that the child can attend the school.

A handicapped child who is a long-stay hospital patient can receive hospital teaching. If the hospital does not have a hospital school, the local education authority can arrange for a teacher to visit the hospital.

Home teaching can be provided if it is not possible to find a suitable special school, or if it is taking a long time to place a handicapped child in a school. Home tuition is not available on a full-time basis. Five half-day sessions per week is the maximum home schooling that is usually provided.

Some types of handicaps and their special problems

A *spastic* or *cerebral palsied* child is one who has suffered brain damage before, during or immediately after birth. The part of the brain that controls movement is affected, and this can result in paralysis of the limbs or an inability to control their movement. The degree of brain damage can vary and some spastic children are able to attend ordinary schools.

If a ***physically handicapped*** child is so disabled that mobility is seriously impaired, then a wheelchair or other piece of apparatus may be needed. This can cause many problems, and ordinary staircases, steps and doorways become impossible obstacles. Ramps, special lifting devices and widened doorways with easily-opened doors have to be made. Lavatories also have to be suitably modified to allow a crippled child easy access.

The orange badge scheme gives disabled drivers or drivers with disabled passengers, special parking concessions. The orange badges, which are issued by the local authority, can be displayed on cars and other vehicles. This sign can also be used to indicate wide lifts in department stores, shopping centres, multi-storey car parks, etc., and is also displayed on public lavatories that are suitably adapted for the physically handicapped.

A ***blind*** or partially sighted child can be helped to become independent by being in an environment that does not change. Furniture should be kept in the same position, so that he can quickly become accustomed to the lay-out of each room. This prevents accidents and helps a blind child to gain confidence in his own ability to negotiate obstacles. Furniture should be firm and sturdy, and not easily knocked over. Sharp edges, loose mats and breakable ornaments should be avoided.

A blind or partially sighted child may be able to attend an ordinary school, if special equipment and facilities are available. Education can also be provided:

a at home;

b in residential schools maintained by the Royal National Institute for the Blind;

c in specially equipped units attached to ordinary schools.

Deafness can usually be detected very early on in life, and if a baby does not seem to be reacting normally to sounds, specialist help should be sought. A deaf child should always be approached from the front, so that he is aware of a presence and is prepared for some type of communication. Simple messages can be conveyed by facial expressions and gestures.

Education for a deaf or hearing-impaired child can be provided:

a at home;

b at special clinics;

c at special day or boarding schools;

d at partial hearing units which are attached to a primary school.

Dyslexia is a disorder of the brain which makes a child unable to recognize the shape of words. A dyslexic child may have reading or writing problems, and difficulty in distinguishing left from right. Letters are often reversed, writing clumsy and cramped, and there is difficulty in spelling. A dyslexic child can be helped:

a by remedial teaching;

b by being taught to read phonetically instead of by the look-and-say method;

c by special courses run by the British Dyslexia Association (18, The Circus, Bath).

Aphasia is a severe speech disorder. An aphasic child is unable to talk even though he can hear clearly. He cannot express ideas in words. An aphasic child can be helped:

a by being encouraged to play with other children;

b by dressing up and pretending to be somebody else;

c by "singing" games;

d by playing with puppets or using mime and drama as a medium for expressing his ideas;

e by being taught to lip read and recognize phonetically spelled words and pictures.

Autism is a disorder of the brain which makes a child unable to respond, communicate or co-operate with other people. An autistic child is prone to sudden bursts of nervous activity and temper tantrums. He is restless and unable to concentrate. An autistic child responds to communications which are directed away from him. He is unhappy and restless when addressed face to face. Music and movement therapy can be helpful, and an autistic child will enjoy playing with puppets, and using mime and drama for self-expression. An autistic child will benefit from mixing and playing with children who have other types of handicap. Special education and treatment can be provided in:

    a the home;

    b day centres for the autistic child;

    c a residential school;

    d a special hospital.

The National Society for Autistic Children (1A, Golders Green Road, London NW11) will offer advice and literature on autism.

Mongolism can be detected at birth. It is a severe form of mental handicap which slows down development. A mongol child is loving, sympathetic and full of mischief, and will benefit from mixing with children who have other types of handicap.

Any young child with a special educational need can be helped by:

    a having his specific disability detected early in life;

    b being given nursery education in a playgroup, nursery school or nursery class;

    c being encouraged to mix with normal children as much as possible;

    d being surrounded with stimulation, e.g. toys, books, music and fun activities;

    e having a loving and secure family background in which he can feel equal to any normal brothers and sisters;

    f being encouraged to be as active, mobile and independent as his handicap allows.

It should always be remembered that a physically handicapped child may be quite normal, mentally and emotionally. He does not want sympathy but desperately needs to be treated as a normal person who happens to have physical limitations.

The problems faced by a family with a handicapped child

The physical and emotional demands of coping with a handicapped child can lead to illness, depression and tensions within a family. Parents may suffer from a feeling of guilt, believing that through carelessness, ignorance or accident they in some way contributed to their child's disability. This may make them try to over-compensate for the handicap, and become too protective or possessive. They may feel obliged to devote all their time and energy to a handicapped child, at the risk of neglecting other members of the family and their own health.

Other children in the family may find it difficult to accept that their brother or sister is different and cannot play and behave like them.

There can be financial problems if furniture and buildings have to be specially adapted to cope with a specific disability, or if specialized equipment has to be bought and maintained. Additional help may be needed in the home to allow the parents to cope with the everyday problems and special needs of their child, and to offer some relief when constant supervision is necessary.

Some families are unable to have holidays or plan for any leisure activities because of the problems these would entail for a handicapped child. BREAK (20, Hooks Hill Road, Sheringham, Norfolk) is an organization which provides holidays and residential care for handicapped children, thus giving a much needed rest to tired and overworked parents.

If special schooling is recommended and a child has to board away from home, there may be added emotional and physical problems, such as:

> *a* the fear that a young child may be homesick and not able to cope with life away from his family;
>
> *b* the fear that in splitting up the family, a handicapped child will lose his sense of identity and feel rejected;
>
> *c* the physical and financial demands involved in travelling to visit a handicapped child.

Living in a stress situation

A **stress situation** can be described as one which makes a child feel unhappy, insecure or inadequate. It may be caused by problems:

at home

e.g. a death;
neglect or cruelty;
the breakdown of a marriage;
continual tension between parents;
the separation, divorce or re-marriage of parents;
poverty or financial hardship;
the illness or mental instability of a parent;
an inability to live up to parents' expectations.

at school

e.g. a learning difficulty;
an unhappy relationship with friends or teachers;
bullying.

in the immediate environment

e.g. living in a depressed or deprived area;
living in a block of high-rise flats;
an inability to cope with life in a multi-racial society.

When a child lives in a stress situation he may become emotionally disturbed. This can show itself as:

a violent, aggressive and disruptive behaviour;

b repeated truancy from school;

c regressive developmental behaviour such as temper tantrums, lying and lack of bladder control;

d delinquency, such as stealing, "mugging", football hooliganism and the vandalizing of public property;

e a complete withdrawal from other people;

f peculiar nervous habits and obsessions.

An emotionally disturbed child can be helped to cope with a stress situation by being encouraged to talk about his problem. In this way he can learn to understand his own feelings and come to terms with them.

A child receives his moral and social values from his parents and from his environment. If a child is brought up in an unhappy home situation or in a depressed area, his code of behaviour will be influenced by his own experiences. If he is subjected to harsh, unjust treatment at home, he is unlikely to be considerate in his dealings with other people, and if he lives in an area where personal possessions are unimportant, he cannot be expected to respect public property.

Schools can do much to help raise the standard of life in depressed areas.

a They can try to compensate for the environment's lack of moral and social training.

b They can surround a child with colour, play equipment, play space, books and pictures, and give ample opportunities for music, movement, drama and self-expression activities.

c Pastoral care and home liaison teachers can try to help with family problems and difficult home circumstances.

d Schools can try to provide a secure, stable and caring environment for a child.

e They can provide out-of-school facilities and organized activities to take a child off the streets.

f They can help to foster good community relations by running crèches and playgroups, involving a child in old people's aid schemes and encouraging him to respect public property.

In an area where high-rise blocks of flats are common, it is especially important for a school to provide space and play equipment to compensate for a child's restricted home environment. School bands and lively games sessions can allow a child to express himself freely, without being inhibited by cramped conditions and fear of disturbing the neighbours. School trips to adventure playparks, the country, the swimming baths, the theatre and historical buildings can all help to widen a child's environment. Living in a stress situation is one of the causes of backwardness.

The backward child

Backwardness is a handicap that is not caused by a major bodily disability. It can be produced by:

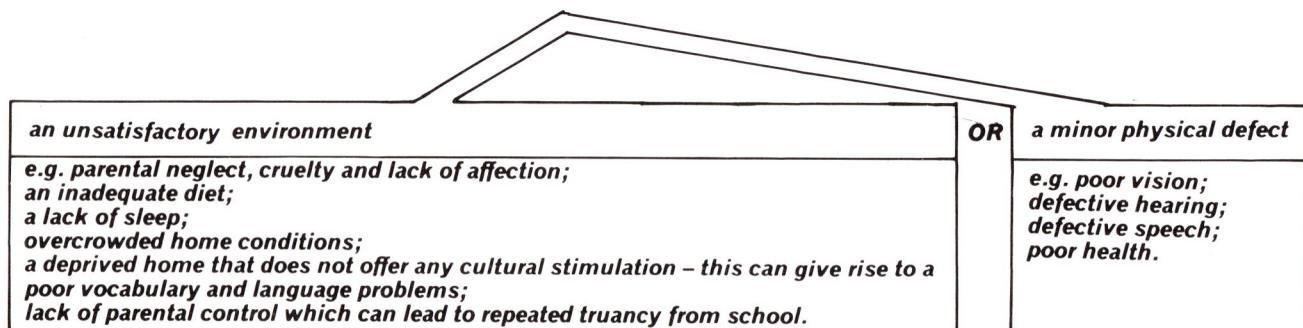

an unsatisfactory environment	OR	a minor physical defect
e.g. parental neglect, cruelty and lack of affection; *an inadequate diet;* *a lack of sleep;* *overcrowded home conditions;* *a deprived home that does not offer any cultural stimulation – this can give rise to a poor vocabulary and language problems;* *lack of parental control which can lead to repeated truancy from school.*		*e.g. poor vision;* *defective hearing;* *defective speech;* *poor health.*

A backward child can be educated in:
  a a small remedial group, class or stream in an ordinary school;
  b an E.S.N. (educationally sub-normal) school;
  c a special training centre for the severely sub-normal.
The National Elfrida Rathbone Society (83, Mosley Street, Manchester M2 3LG) is a voluntary organization which specializes in social work for the educationally handicapped child and those handicapped by their environment.

One-parent families

There has been a rapid increase in the number of one-parent families. This can be explained by:

the changing attitude towards illegitimacy which allows more unmarried mothers to keep their children

the improved Social Services Department which helps combat poverty, social hardship and the employment problems of one-parent families

the increase in the divorce and separation rate

the formation of voluntary social service groups which offer guidance, legal advice and information specifically for one-parent families

It can be argued that a child is better off living with one stable parent who is happy, than being with two parents in a home where there is constant tension and conflict. An insecure and strained home environment can lead to emotional difficulties. However, a child from a one-parent family can suffer, if:

a the strain of coping single-handed makes the parent unhappy, depressed or neurotic;

b there is not sufficient money to provide for the "luxuries" of life such as regular holidays, birthday and Christmas treats;

c the single parent has a job which does not fit in with school hours, and the child has to return to an empty home each night;

d there is inadequate supervision during the long school holidays, because the parent dare not risk having time off work.

Here are some useful addresses for one-parent families.

1 The National Council for One-Parent Families, 255 Kentish Town Road, London NW5 2LX

2 The Scottish Council for Single Parents, 44 Albany Street, Edinburgh EH1 3QR

3 Gingerbread (a self-help group for one-parent families), 35 Wellington Street, London WC2

4 Families Need Fathers, 23 Holmes Road, Kentish Town, London NW5

5 Singlehanded Ltd., 68 Lewes Road, Haywards Heath, Sussex

The coloured immigrant and the multi-racial child

Although coloured immigrants have been present in Britain for centuries, it is only since the early 1950s, when Commonwealth immigrants flowed into this country from India, Pakistan and the West Indies, that the colour question has become a problem.

The coloured immigrants who came to Britain tended to settle in the larger cities because there were more jobs available in these areas. Relatives and friends, who followed, preferred to live near their compatriots, with whom they had more in common, and so certain areas of Britain became heavily populated with coloured immigrants.

In the 1960s, racial tension grew steadily worse and discrimination in housing and employment was widespread.

The children born to these coloured immigrants have had to grow up in a multi-racial society. People of a different race have:

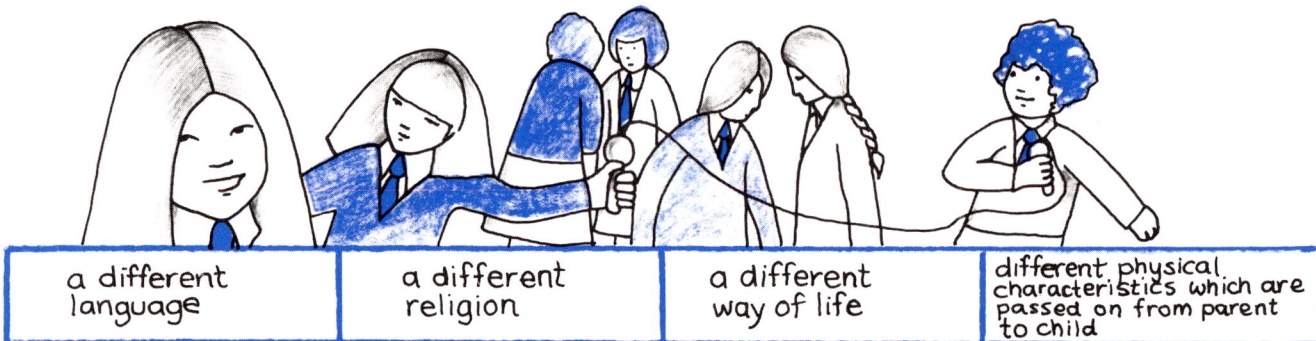

| a different language | a different religion | a different way of life | different physical characteristics which are passed on from parent to child |

It is not easy to grow up amongst people who look, talk, dress, think and behave differently from oneself and there is growing evidence that the children of coloured immigrants are not doing as well at school as might have been expected. Many city schools provide special classes for coloured immigrant children who speak English badly or not at all. There are television and radio programmes which cater for racial minorities, and many local radio stations provide programmes for the ethnic minorities in their region. These programmes try to help the coloured immigrant to understand the English language and the British way of life.

It is important to encourage inter-racial mixing in the pre-school period, so that a young child grows up to accept and understand people of a different race and culture.

Problems can arise when the older generation of immigrant clings to his own racial culture and traditions, but sees his children growing up with a different set of values.

The Commission for Racial Equality was set up to eliminate discrimination because of colour, race or nationality. It seeks to give equal opportunities in education, housing, services and employment to people of different racial groups, and to help foster good inter-racial relationships.

Here are some of the local bodies who will help and advise on racial problems.

1 The Citizens Advice Bureaux
2 Community Relations Councils
3 Legal Advice Centres
4 Local Employment Offices or Job Centres
5 The Race Relations Employment Advisory Service (Department of Employment)

Think and Do

1. Explain why there has been a rapid increase in the number of one-parent families. What special problems are faced by these families? Where can a single parent go for help and advice?

2. List the difficulties involved in bringing up young children in a block of high-rise flats.

3. Copy the diagram into your notebook. Underneath write a few sentences to explain the meaning of the sign.

4. Write a paragraph about each of the following:

a. special schools for the handicapped child;

b. the effect on a child of stress situations within a family;

c. the multi-racial child.

5. List some of the causes of backwardness.

6. How can a blind child be helped to come to terms with his disability?

7. Copy the following diagram into your notebook. In each of the boxes, write a suitable sentence.

EDUCATING CHILDREN WITH SPECIAL NEEDS

In an ordinary school	In a special school (day or boarding)	In a hospital school	In the home

8. How can a good school compensate for a deprived environment?

9. Write *two* sentences about each of the following:

a. dyslexia;

b. autism;

c. aphasia;

d. cerebral palsy;

e. mongolism.

10. What special problems are faced by families with a handicapped child?